Collins

INTERNATIONAL PRIMARY MATHS

Student's Book 2

William Collins' dream of knowledge for all began with the publication of his first book in 1819.
A self-educated mill worker, he not only enriched millions of lives, but also founded a flourishing publishing house. Today, staying true to this spirit, Collins books are packed with inspiration, innovation and practical expertise. They place you at the centre of a world of possibility and give you exactly what you need to explore it.

Collins. Freedom to teach.

An imprint of HarperCollins*Publishers*
The News Building
1 London Bridge Street
London
SE1 9GF

Browse the complete Collins catalogue at www.collins.co.uk

10 9 8 7 6 5 4 3 2 1

ISBN 978-0-00-815984-9

Lisa Jarmin and Ngaire Orsborn assert their moral rights to be identified as the authors of this work.

British Library Cataloguing in Publication Data
A catalogue record for this publication is available from the British Library.

Commissioned by Fiona McGlade
Series editor Peter Clarke
Project editor Kate Ellis
Project managed by Emily Hooton
Developed by Joan Miller and Tracy Thomas
Edited by Tanya Solomons
Proofread by Catherine Dakin
Cover design by Ink Tank
Cover artwork by Aflo Co. Ltd./Alamy Stock Photo
Internal design by Ken Vail Graphic Design
Typesetting by Ken Vail Graphic Design
Illustrations by Ken Vail Graphic Design, Advocate Art, Beehive Illustration and QBS
Production by Lauren Crisp

Printed and bound by Grafica Veneta S. P. A.

Photo acknowledgements

Every effort has been made to trace copyright holders. Any omission will be rectified at the first opportunity.

Front cover and title page Aflo Co. Ltd./Alamy Stock Photo, p1 matimix/Shutterstock, p27l imagineerinx/Shutterstock, p27r Peter Zijlstra/Shutterstock, p73l Sergio Stakhnyk/Shutterstock, p73c fon thachakul/Shutterstock, p73r rin-k/Shutterstock, p73cl Molodec/Shutterstock, p73bl Fleckstone/Shutterstock, p73bm ArtLight Production/Shutterstock, p73br drpnncpptak/Shutterstock, p77bc Vladislav Gajic/Shutterstock, p77b Palokha Tetiana/Shutterstock, p77tr Shahril KHMD/Shutterstock, p81 uk atrasat/Shutterstock, p84tl Pix11/Shutterstock, p84tr grossishut/Shutterstock, p84tcl PhotoStockImage/Shutterstock, p84bcl Neamov/Shutterstock, p84bcr StudioSmart/Shutterstock, p84br Lance Sagar/Shutterstock, p84bl Photo Image/Shutterstock, p95t Syda Productions/Shutterstock, p95c Dancake/Shutterstock, p95b pritsana/Shutterstock, p98t Eric Isselee/Shutterstock, p99t Yann hubert/Shutterstock, p99tcl 5 second Studio/Shutterstock, p99tc Gajic Dragan/Shutterstock, p99c Mega Pixel/Shutterstock, p99bc Neamov/Shutterstock, p99bl Natan86/Shutterstock, p99cl litchima/Shutterstock, p99cr jaroslava V/Shutterstock, p99br Hayati Kayhan/Shutterstock, p102tl Sittiporn Masantear/Shutterstock, p102tc Kletr/Shutterstock, p102tr ana8pana/Shutterstock, p102cr (a) Evan Lorne/Shutterstock, p102cr (b) s-ts/Shutterstock, p102cr (c) Davydenko Yuliia/Shutterstock, p102cl (a and b) Piotr Marcinski/Shutterstock, p102bl Africa Studio/Shutterstock, p102br Viktorija Reuta/Shutterstock, p103tc topseller/Shutterstock, p104 picturepartners/Shutterstock, p106tl konzeptm/Shutterstock, p106tcl s-ts/Shutterstock, p106tcr and bc (b) Mariyana M/Shutterstock, p106tr impido/Shutterstock, p106c (a) akoistock/Shutterstock, p106c (b) Fotofermer/Shutterstock, p106c (c) anaken2012/Shutterstock, p106bc (a) Gts/Shutterstock, p106bc (c) posteriori/Shutterstock, p106b (a) Barnaby Chambers/Shutterstock, p106b (b) Alexandru Nika/Shutterstock, p107bl Davidson Lentz/Shutterstock, p107br Gts/Shutterstock, p108 racorn/Shutterstock, p112t Anneka/Shutterstock, p112c Rob Marmion/Shutterstock, p112b igor kisselev/Shutterstock, p113t Gts/Shutterstock, p118tl Gelpi JM/Shutterstock, p118tr Stuart Monk/Shutterstock, p119l Early Spring/Shutterstock, p119r Veronica Louro/Shutterstock, p120 Zurijeta/Shutterstock.

Contents

Number

Geometry

Measure

Handling data

Lesson 1: Numbers to 100

- Count, read and write numbers to 100

Key words
- number
- numeral
- count

Discover

Can you read and write the numbers?

Learn

0 zero
1 one
2 two
3 three
4 four
5 five
6 six
7 seven
8 eight
9 nine

10 ten
20 twenty
30 thirty
40 forty
50 fifty
60 sixty
70 seventy
80 eighty
90 ninety
100 hundred

Lesson 2: Counting on and back in steps

- Count in 2s, 5s and 10s

Key words
- count
- skip-count
- twos
- fives
- tens

Discover

2, 4, 6, 8, 10, ...

Learn

You say the shaded numbers when you skip-count in 2s, 5s and 10s.

2s

1	2	3	4	5	6	7	8	9	10
11	12	13	14	15	16	17	18	19	20
21	22	23	24	25	26	27	28	29	30
31	32	33	34	35	36	37	38	39	40
41	42	43	44	45	46	47	48	49	50

5s

1	2	3	4	5	6	7	8	9	10
11	12	13	14	15	16	17	18	19	20
21	22	23	24	25	26	27	28	29	30
31	32	33	34	35	36	37	38	39	40
41	42	43	44	45	46	47	48	49	50

10s

1	2	3	4	5	6	7	8	9	10
11	12	13	14	15	16	17	18	19	20
21	22	23	24	25	26	27	28	29	30
31	32	33	34	35	36	37	38	39	40
41	42	43	44	45	46	47	48	49	50

Lesson 3: **Counting many objects (1)**

- Count up to 100 objects
- Count objects in groups of 2, 5 or 10

Key words
- group
- count
- twos
- fives
- tens

Discover

These beads have been put into groups of 2s, 5s and 10s.

2

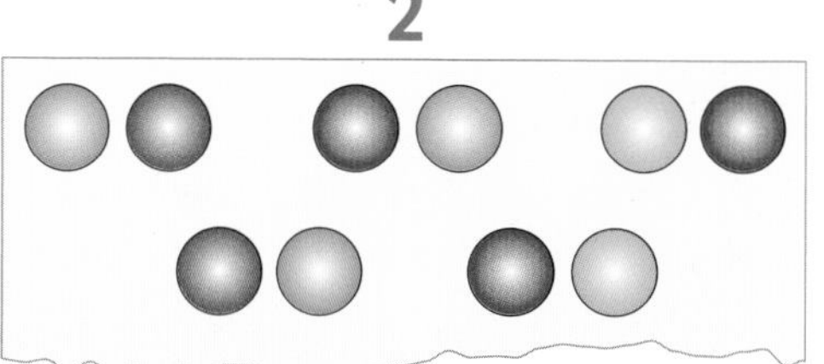

5

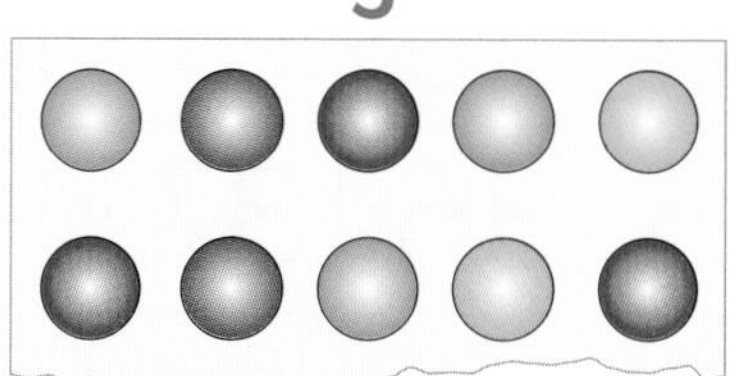

10

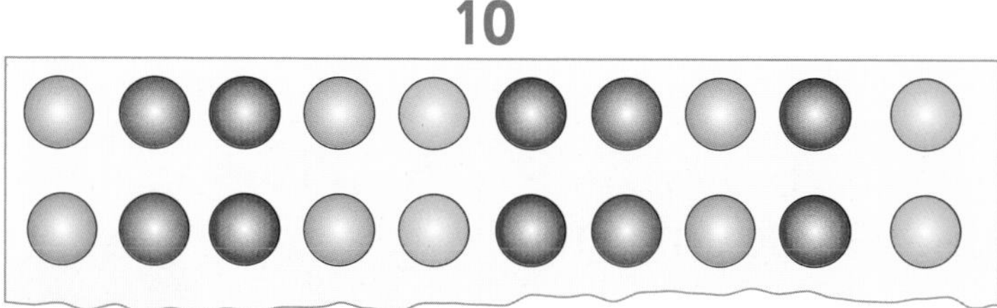

Learn

You can put objects into groups of 2, 5 or 10 to make them easier to count.

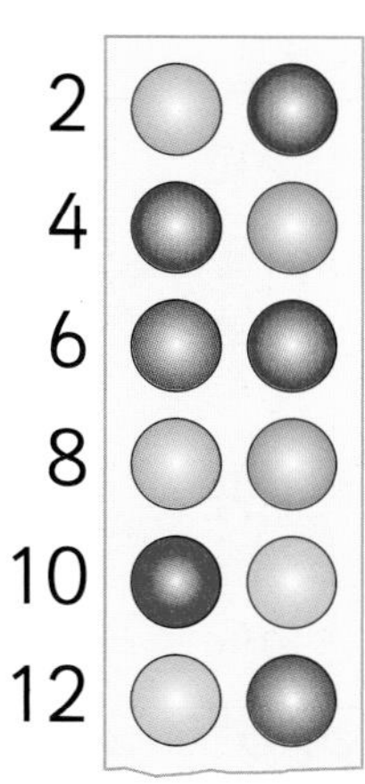

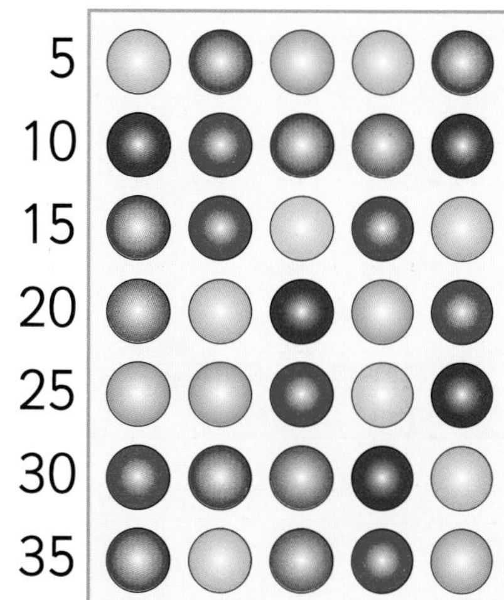

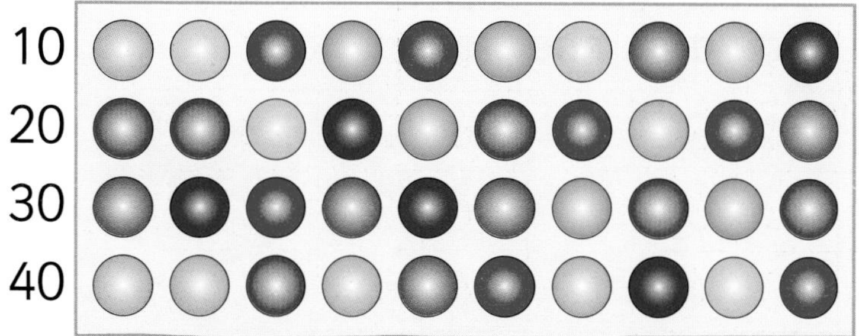

Lesson 4: **1 or 10 more or less**

- Find 1 or 10 more or less than a number

Key words
- more
- less

Discover

10 less (arrow to 15)

13	14	15	16	17
23	24	25	26	27
33	34	35	36	37

1 less (arrow to 24) 1 more (arrow to 26)

10 more (arrow to 35)

Learn

To find 1 more than a number, count on 1.

1 more than 25:

To find 1 less than a number, count back 1.

1 less than 25:

To find 10 more than a number, count on in 10s.

10 more than 25:

To find 10 less than a number, count back in 10s.

10 less than 25:

Lesson 5: **Finding numbers**

- Say a number that falls between 2 other numbers
- Place a 2-digit number on a number line

Key words
- tens
- between
- more
- less

Discover

The red arrow is pointing halfway between 20 and 30, where 25 would be.

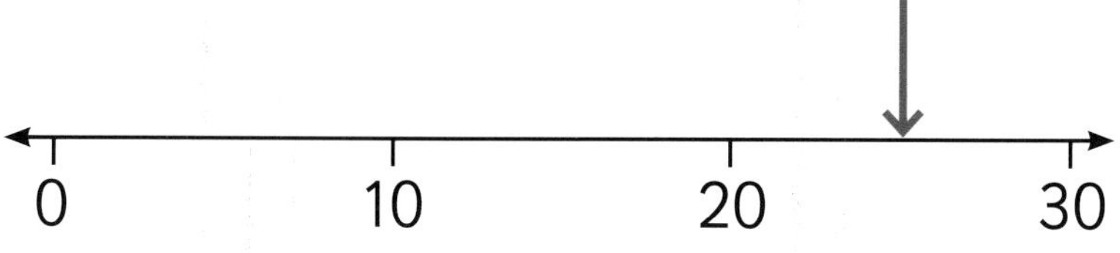

Learn

These numbers lie between 20 and 30.

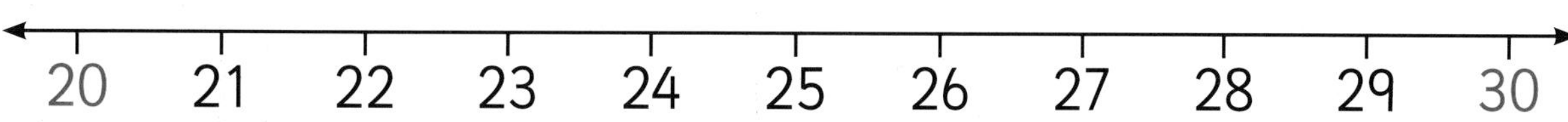

To work out where to put 23 on a number line, first find 25 at the halfway point. Then count back to 23.

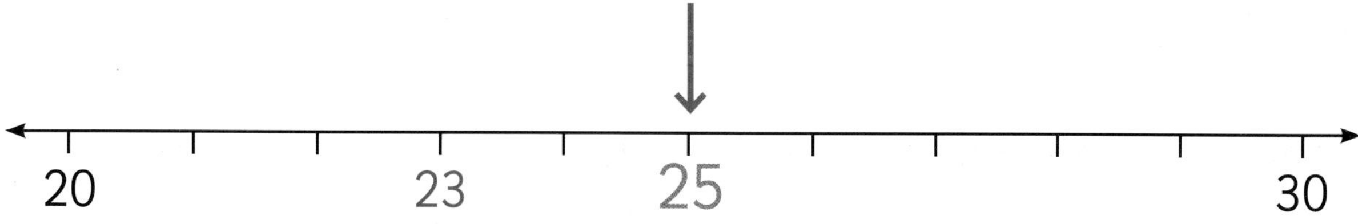

Say a number that falls between 50 and 60.

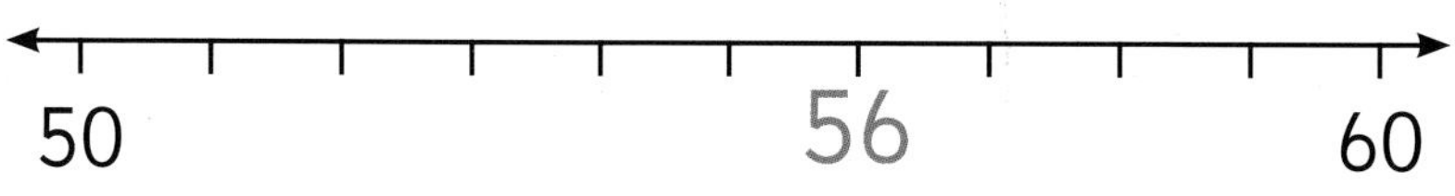

Lesson 6: **Rounding numbers (1)**

- Round 2-digit numbers to the nearest 10

Key words
- tens
- round up
- round down

Discover

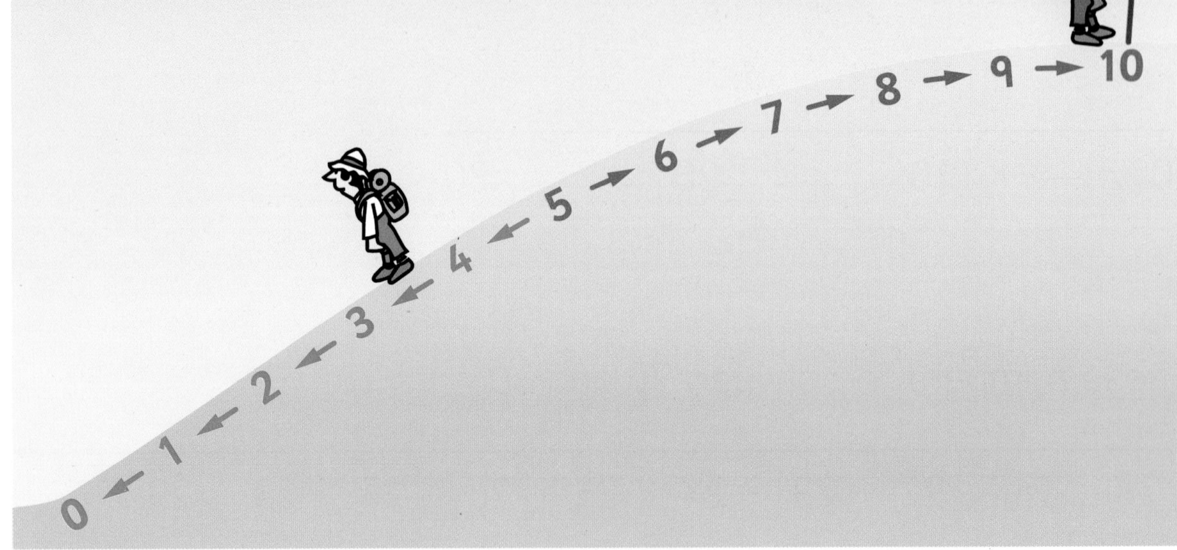

Learn

1, 2, 3, 4 round DOWN to the nearest 10.

5, 6, 7, 8, 9 round UP to the nearest 10.

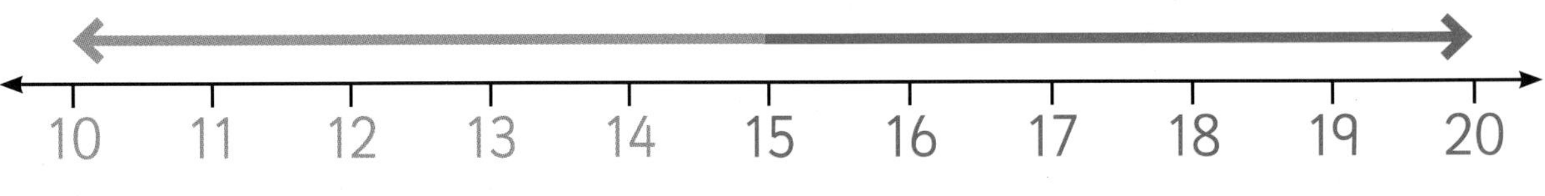

Example

Round 26 to the nearest 10.

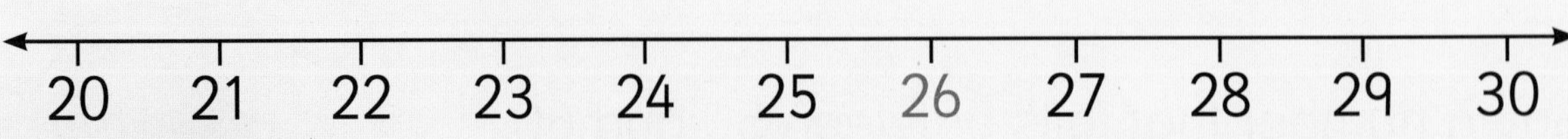

26 rounds up to 30.

Lesson 7: **Ordinal numbers**

- Use ordinal numbers

Key words
- **ordinal numbers**
- **first/second/third/fourth/fifth/sixth/seventh/eighth/ninth/tenth**

Discover

The days of the month are ordinal numbers.

April						
M	**T**	**W**	**T**	**F**	**S**	**S**
1st	2nd	3rd	4th doctors	5th	6th	7th
8th	9th	10th party	11th	12th	13th	14th
15th	16th	17th	18th	19th	20th	21st
22nd	23rd	24th	25th	26th	27th	28th
29th	30th					

Learn

Ordinal numbers put people, objects or events in order.

1st	2nd	3rd	4th	5th	6th	7th	8th	9th	10th

first	second	third	fourth	fifth	sixth	seventh	eighth	ninth	tenth

Example

Write the order.

1st

2nd

3rd

4th

5th

Lesson 8: **Odd and even numbers**

- Recognise odd and even numbers to 20

Key words
- **odd**
- **even**

Discover

Some of these children's ages are odd and some are even.

Learn

Even numbers end in 0, 2, 4, 6 or 8.

Odd numbers end in 1, 3, 5, 7 or 9.

1	2	3	4	5	6	7	8	9	10	11	12	13	14	15	16	17	18	19	20

Example

Circle the number that should not be in this group.

1, 5, 7, (8), 9

Lesson 1: **Counting many objects (2)**

- Count on and back in ones and tens
- Make groups of objects and count them in 2s, 5s and 10s

Key words
- groups
- skip-count
- ones
- twos
- fives
- tens

Discover

How can you count a large number of objects?

Learn

Put objects into 2s, 5s or 10s to help you count them.

Small amounts can be grouped in 2s.

Medium amounts can be grouped in 5s.

Large amounts can be grouped in 10s.

Lesson 2: **Place value (1)**

- Know how many tens and ones are in a 2-digit number

Key words
- tens
- ones
- partition

Discover

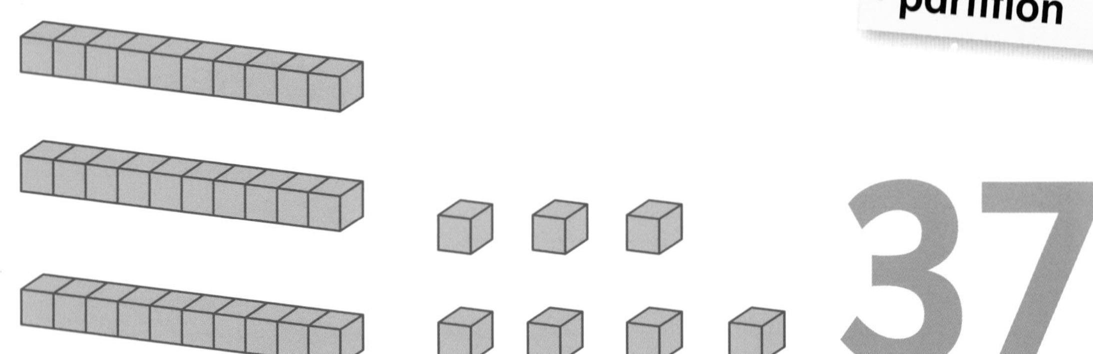

Learn

2-digit numbers are made up of tens and ones.

Tens	Ones
6	3

Lesson 3: **Place value (2)**

- Partition 2-digit numbers into tens and ones

Key words
- tens
- ones
- partition

Discover

23 has been partitioned into 20 and 3.

23

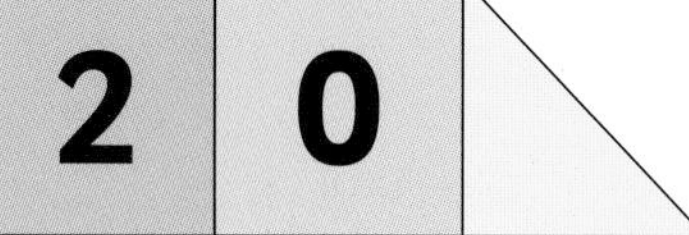

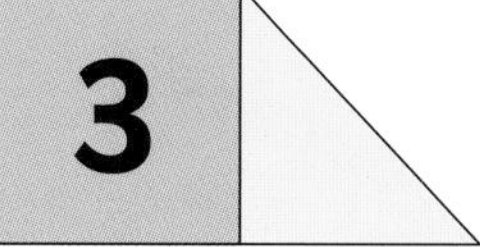

Learn

One way to partition a 2-digit number is to split it into tens and ones.

You can show it like this:

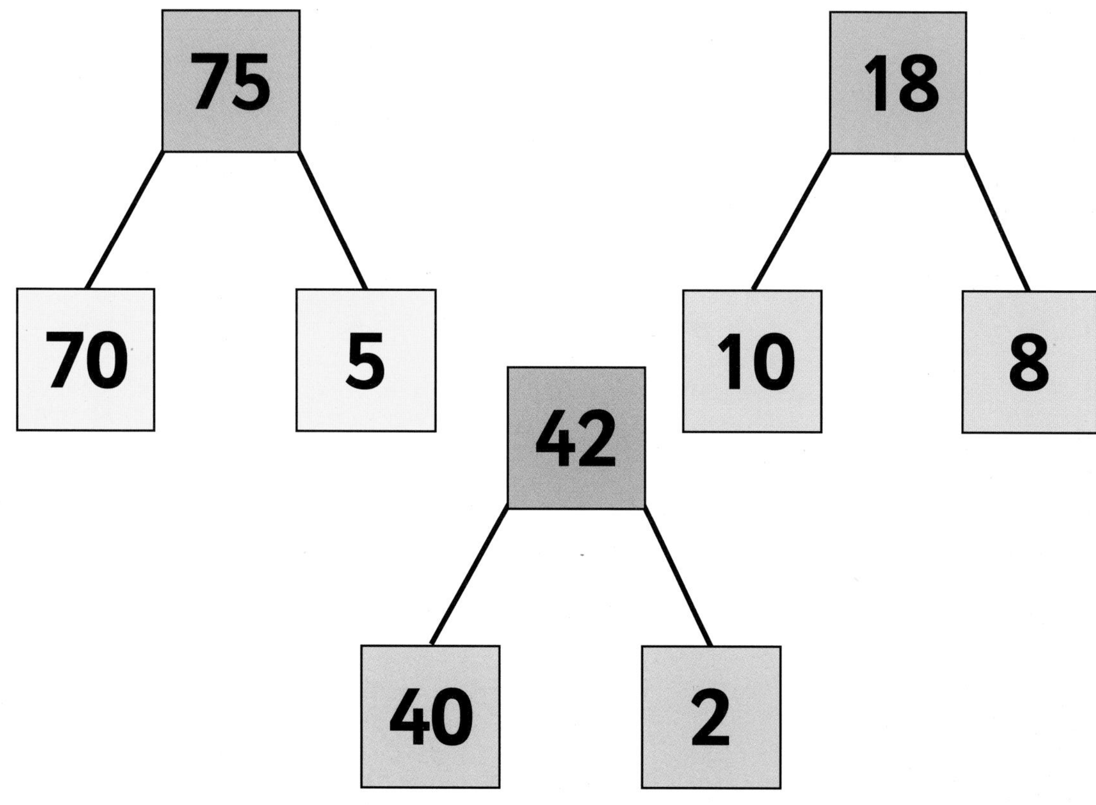

Lesson 4: **Comparing numbers**

- Use the < and > signs to compare two numbers

Key words

- larger
- more
- smaller
- less

Discover

The first snail is smaller than the second snail.

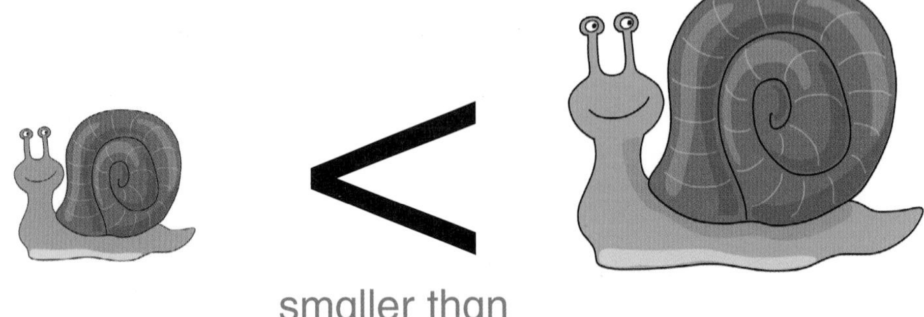

smaller than

The first snail is larger than the second snail.

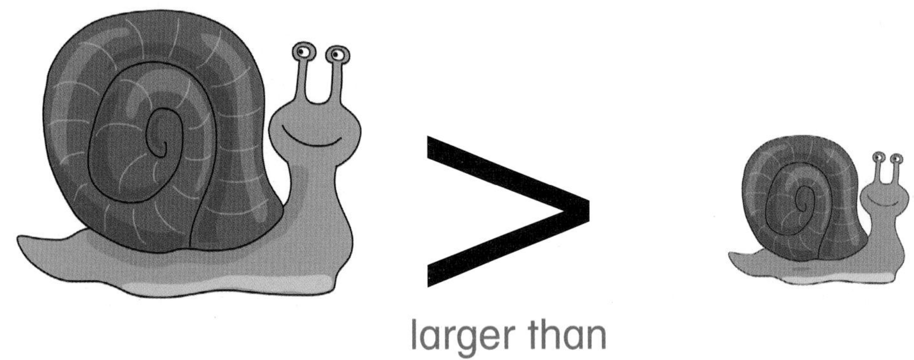

larger than

Learn

You use **<** and **>** between two numbers to show which is the smaller or larger number.

36 < 70 — 36 is smaller than 70.

59 > 48 — 59 is larger than 48.

Lesson 5: Ordering numbers

• Order numbers to 100

Key words
- more
- less
- largest
- smallest
- order

Discover

How do you decide which number is smallest?

Learn

First, look at the tens in each number.

24 57 72 96

24 has the smallest number of tens.

If some or all the numbers have the same number of tens, use the ones to put them in order.

42 55 56 63

Example

Write this set of numbers in order, smallest to largest.

48, 15, 30, 86, 27

15	27	30	48	86

Lesson 6: **Rounding numbers (2)**

- Round 2-digit numbers to the nearest 10

Key words
- tens
- round up
- round down

Discover

Learn

When a number ends in 1, 2, 3 or 4, round it down.

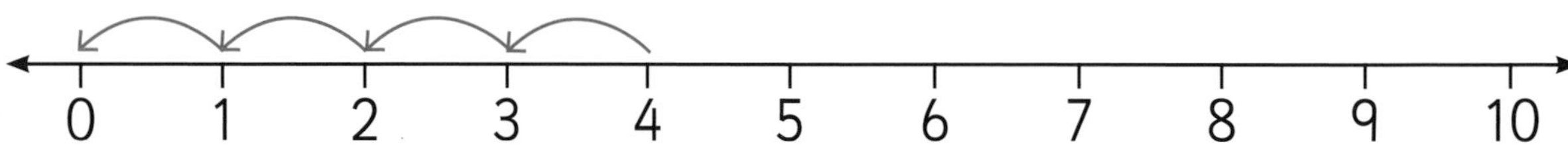

When a number ends in 5, 6, 7, 8 or 9, round it up.

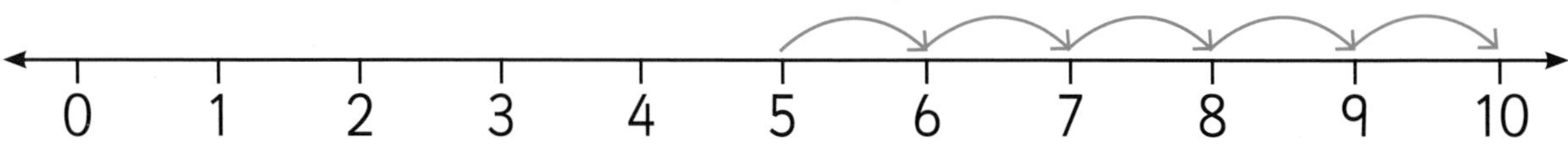

Lesson 7: **Estimating**

- Estimate 'how many' for up to 100 objects

Key words
- estimate
- more
- less
- twos
- fives
- tens

Discover

About how many cubes can you see?

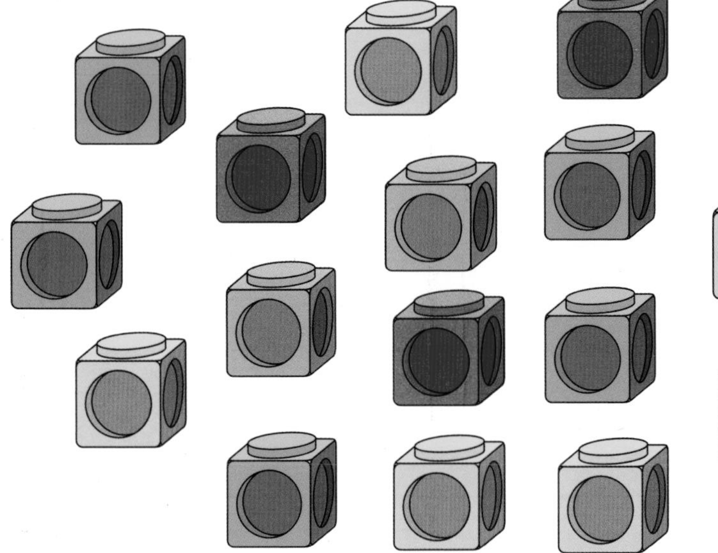

Learn

These amounts of cubes can help to estimate 'how many'.

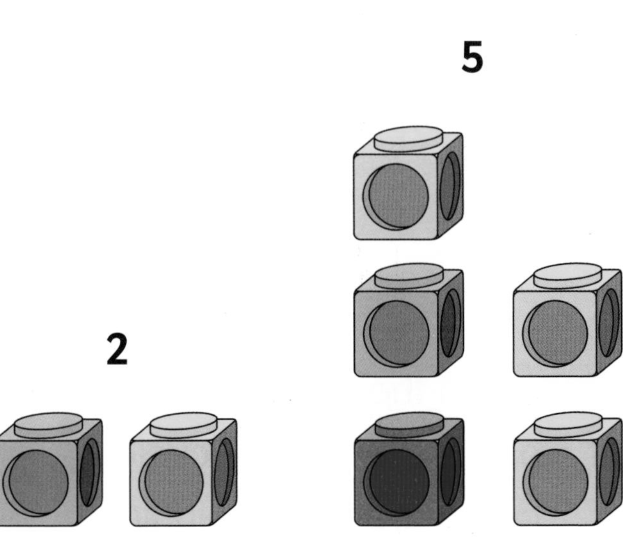

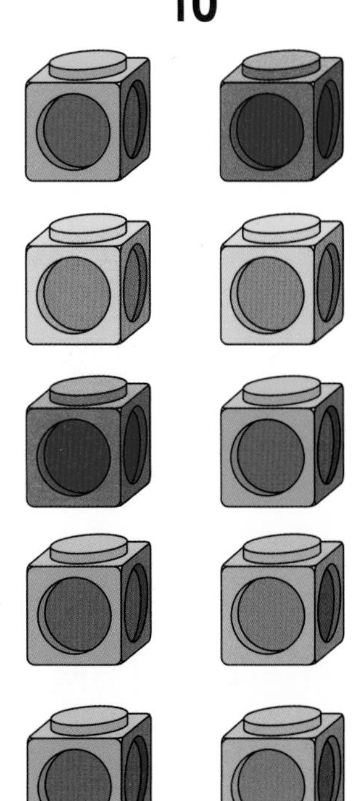

Lesson 8: **Sorting numbers**

- Sort numbers into groups

Key words
- sort
- odd
- even
- tens
- fives
- twos
- multiples

Discover

How have these numbers been sorted?

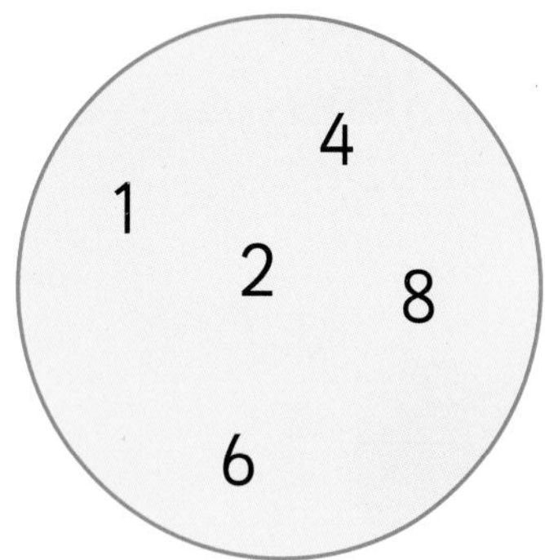

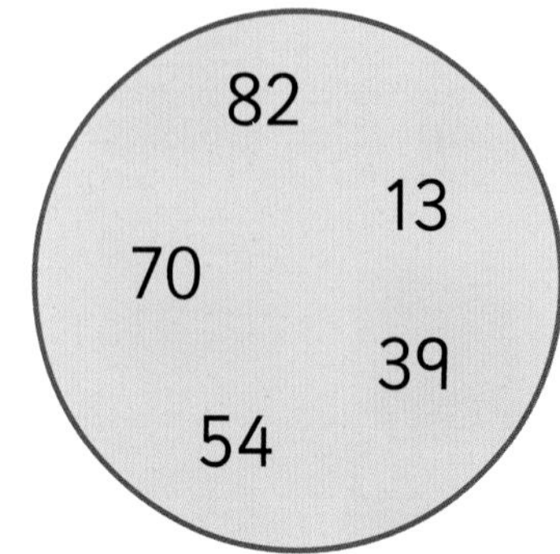

Learn

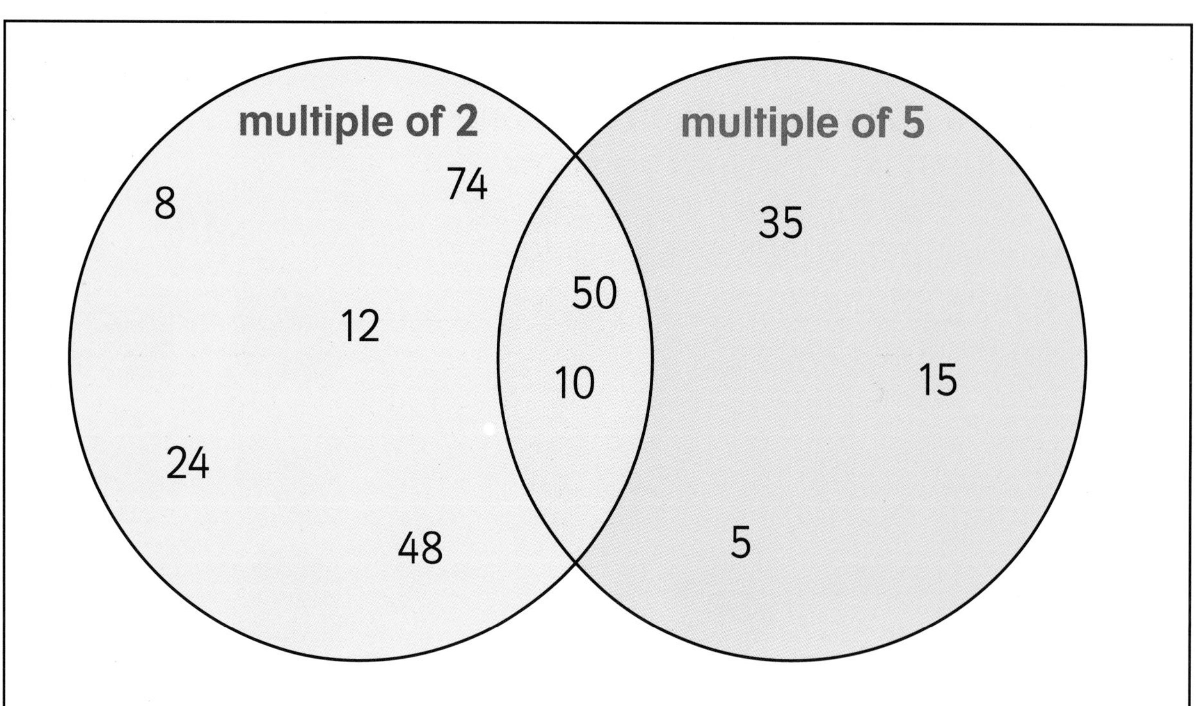

Numbers that are multiples of 2 are in the first circle.
Numbers that are multiples of 5 are in the second circle.
Numbers that are multiples of 2 and 5 are in the middle.

Lesson 1: **Counting in 2s, 5s and 10s**

- Make and continue number patterns by counting in 2s, 5s and 10s

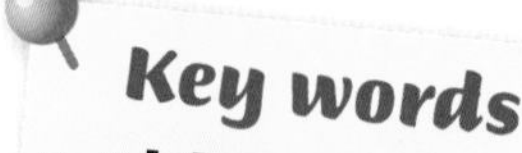

Key words
- skip-count
- patterns
- twos
- fives
- tens

Number

Discover

Misha is thinking of a number pattern that counts on in 2s.

6, 8, 10, 12, ...
What comes next?

Learn

To work out a pattern, count on from one number to the next. This tells you how many to count on between the numbers.

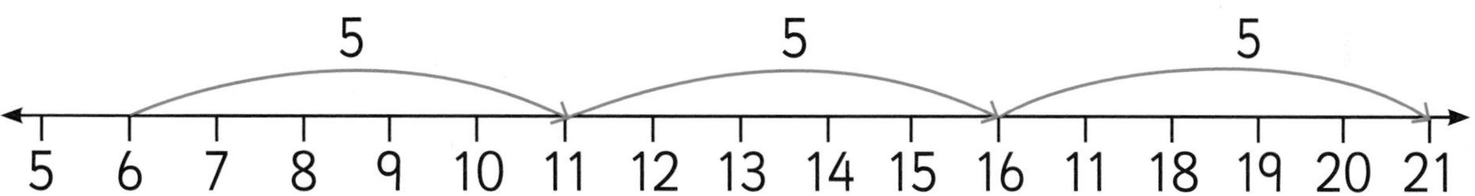

This pattern is counting on in 5s.

Example

Continue the number patterns.

8 10 12 14 16 18 20

Lesson 2: **Counting in constant steps**

- Count on in small constant steps

Key words
- count
- skip-count
- threes
- fours
- patterns

Discover

Sophia is counting in 3s.
Mario is counting in 4s.

3, 6, 9, 12, ...

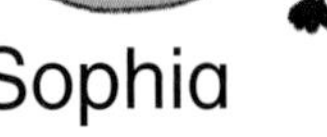

Mario

4, 8, 12, 16, ...

Learn

These are the numbers you say when you count in 3s.

1	2	3	4	5	6	7	8	9	10
11	12	13	14	15	16	17	18	19	20
21	22	23	24	25	26	27	28	29	30

These are the numbers you say when you count in 4s.

1	2	3	4	5	6	7	8	9	10
11	12	13	14	15	16	17	18	19	20
21	22	23	24	25	26	27	28	29	30
31	32	33	34	35	36	37	38	39	40

Example

Skip-count the cherries in 6s:

6 12 18

Lesson 3: **Place value (3)**

- Write a number sentence to partition a 2-digit number

Key words
- tens
- ones
- partition

Discover

Learn

You can write a number sentence to partition a 2-digit number.

Example

Fill in the missing number.

73 = 70 + [3]

Lesson 4: **Comparing and ordering numbers (2)**

- Use the < and > signs to compare two numbers
- Put numbers to 100 in order

Key words
- larger
- smaller
- more
- less

Discover

Putting **<** or **>** between two numbers helps you to compare them.

Learn

Put **<** and **>** between two numbers to show which is smaller and which is larger.

Smallest to largest:
23 < 40

Largest to smallest:
83 > 57

Example

Write these numbers in order, from smallest to largest.

34, 18, 51, 6, 99

6	18	34	51	99

Lesson 1: **Halves**

- Write one half as $\frac{1}{2}$
- Recognise shapes that are divided into halves and shapes that are not

Key words
- **half**
- **halves**
- **equal**

Number

Discover

The paper has been divided into halves.

Learn

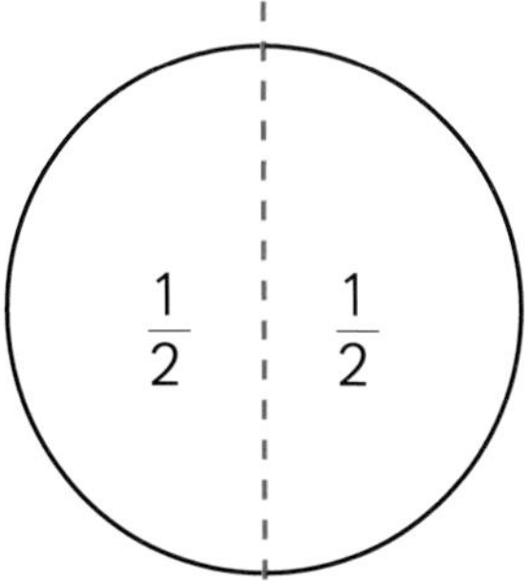

This circle has been divided in half.

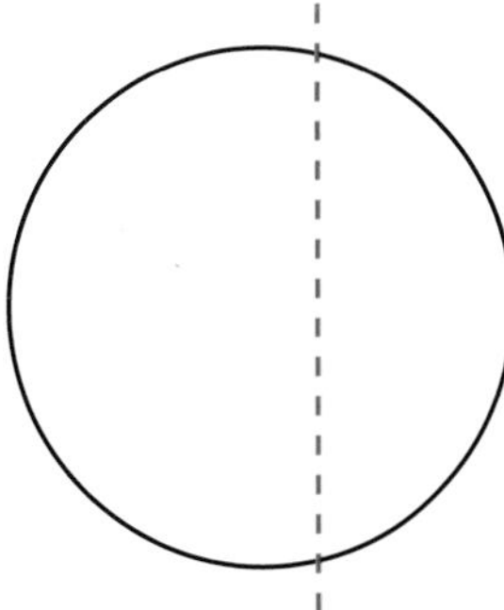

This circle has not been divided in half.

You write one half like this: $\frac{1}{2}$

Example

Colour the shapes that are divided into halves, then label each half $\frac{1}{2}$.

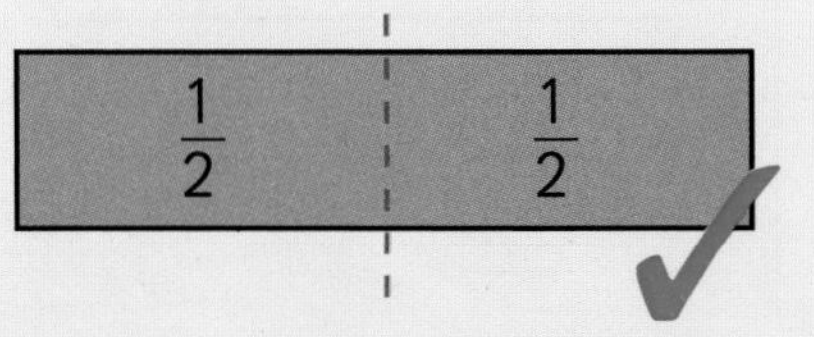

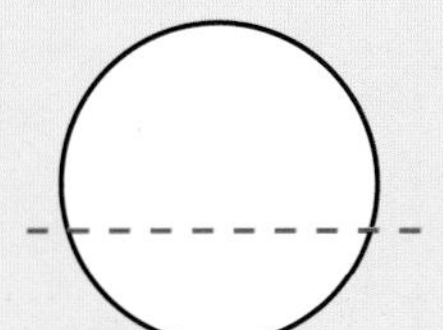

Lesson 2: **Quarters**

- Write one quarter as $\frac{1}{4}$
- Recognise which shapes are divided into quarters and which are not

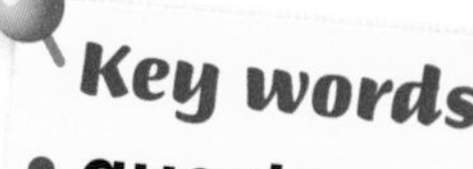

Key words

- **quarters**
- **equal**

Discover

When a shape is divided into 4 equal parts, it is in quarters.

Learn

These squares have been divided into quarters.

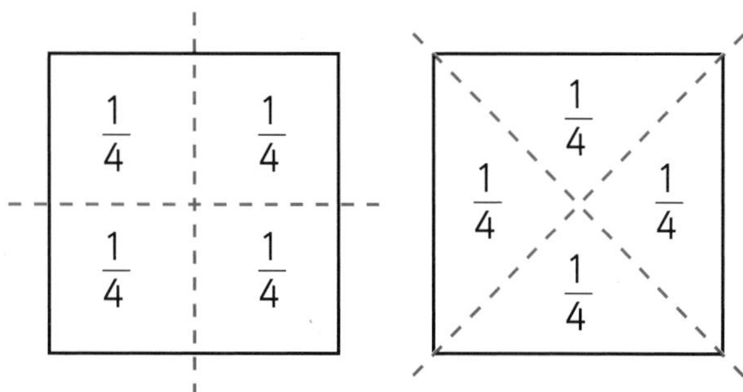

This square has not been divided into quarters.

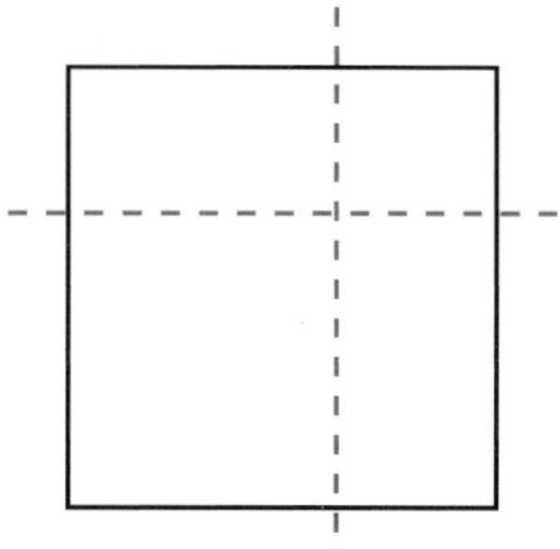

You write one quarter like this: $\frac{1}{4}$

Example

Colour the shapes that are divided into quarters, then label each quarter $\frac{1}{4}$.

$\frac{1}{4}$	$\frac{1}{4}$
$\frac{1}{4}$	$\frac{1}{4}$

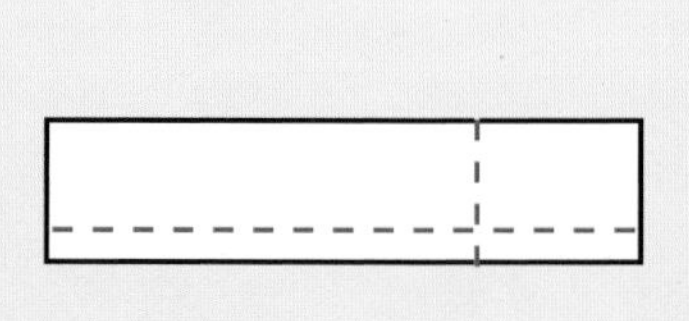

Lesson 3: **Three quarters**

- Recognise and write $\frac{3}{4}$

Key words
- quarters
- three quarters
- equal

Discover

This cake has been divided into quarters.

$\frac{3}{4}$

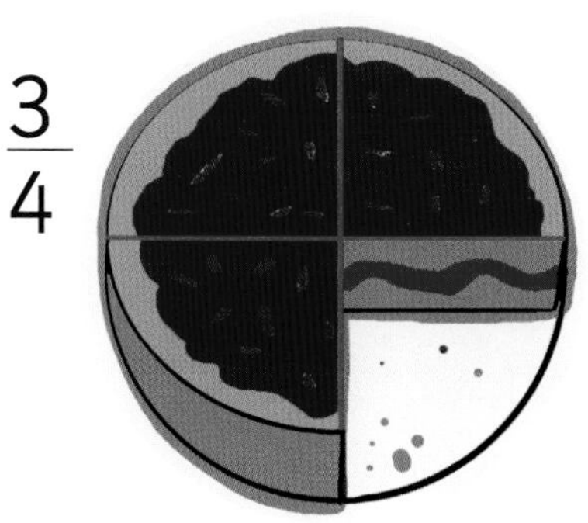

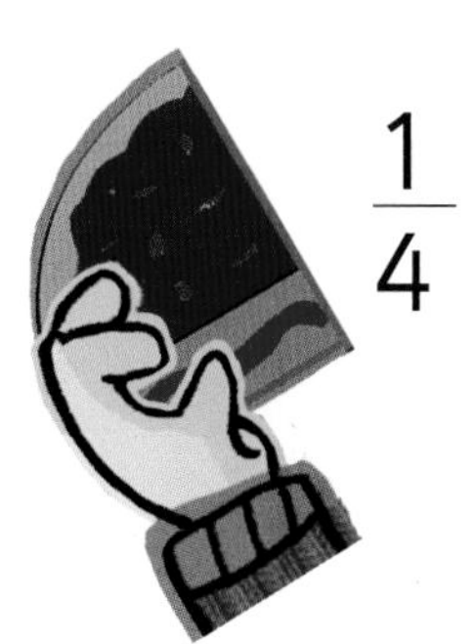

$\frac{1}{4}$

Learn

This square is divided into quarters.
Three quarters are coloured in.

You write three quarters like this: $\frac{3}{4}$

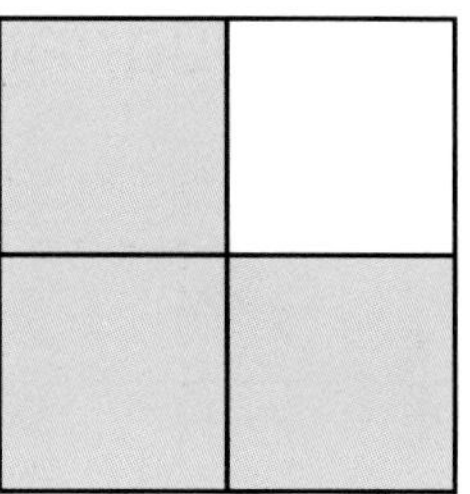

Example

Tick the shape that has three quarters shaded.
Label the shaded area $\frac{3}{4}$ and the unshaded area $\frac{1}{4}$.

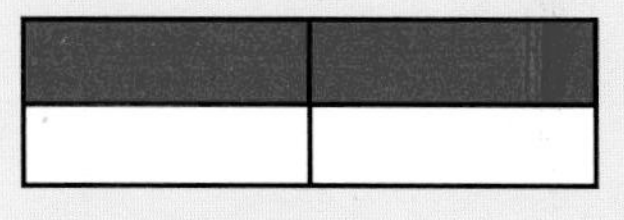

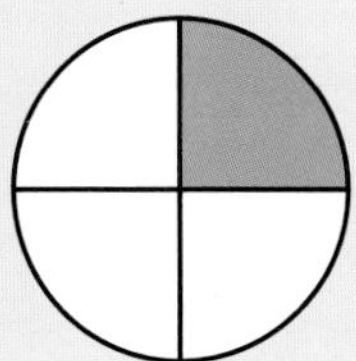

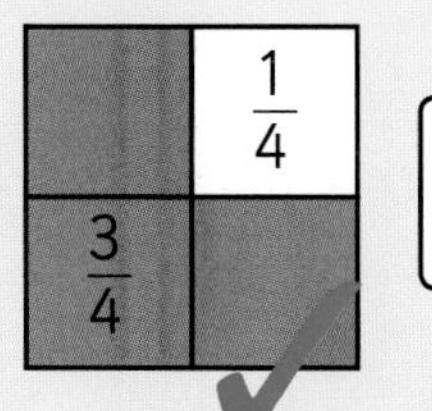

$\frac{3}{4}$

Lesson 4: **Halves and quarters of shapes**

- Find halves and quarters of shapes

Key words
- half
- halves
- quarters
- equal

Discover

You could divide this flag into halves or quarters.

Learn

You can find half of a shape by folding it so that the sides match up, then drawing a line down the fold. To find a quarter, fold it again.

$\frac{1}{4}$

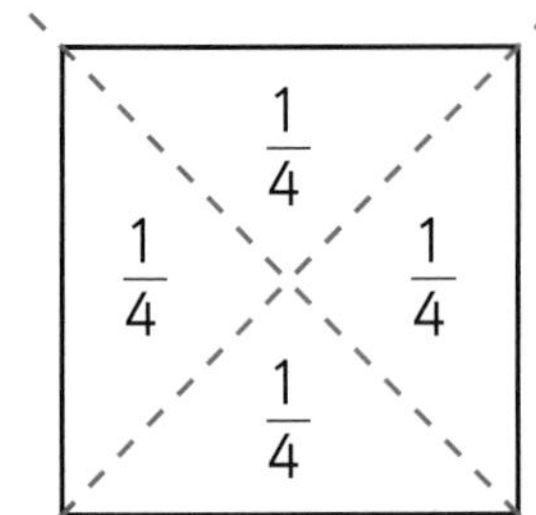

Example

Use a pencil and ruler to divide this shape into halves. Colour one half and label it $\frac{1}{2}$.

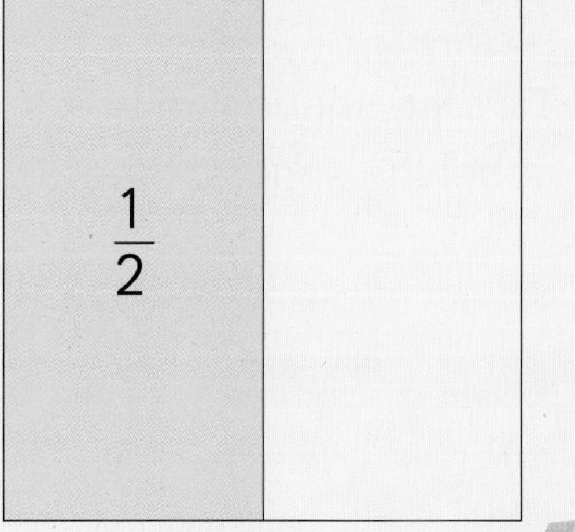

Lesson 5: **Making a whole**

- Recognise that $\frac{2}{2}$ and $\frac{4}{4}$ both make a whole

Key words

- half
- halves
- quarters
- whole
- equal

Discover

This whole pizza has been cut into 4 quarters.

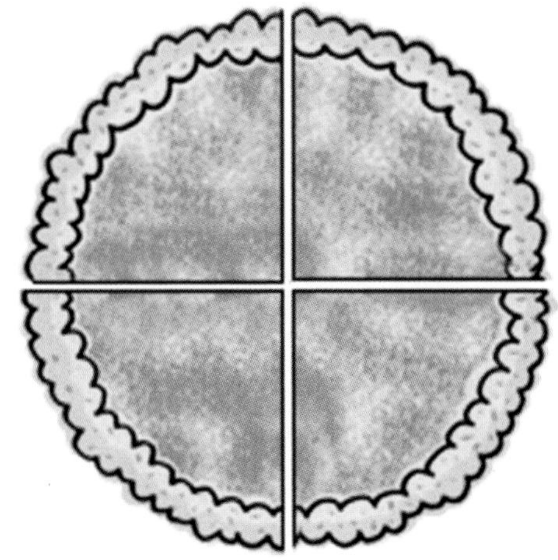

Learn

2 halves ($\frac{2}{2}$) make one whole.

4 quarters ($\frac{4}{4}$) make one whole.

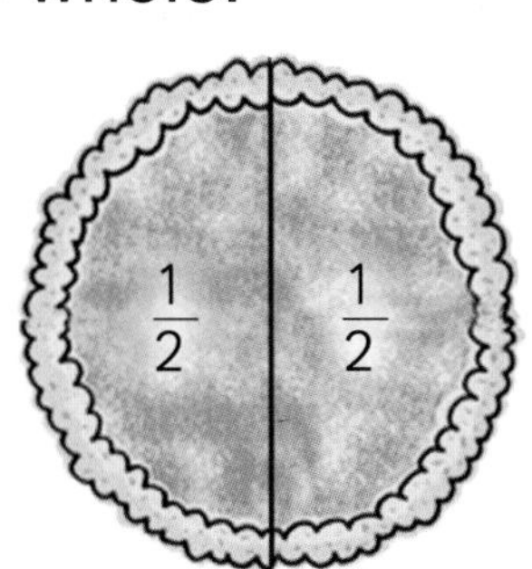

$\frac{1}{4}$ $\frac{1}{4}$ $\frac{1}{4}$ $\frac{1}{4}$

Example

How many more quarters must be shaded to make one whole?

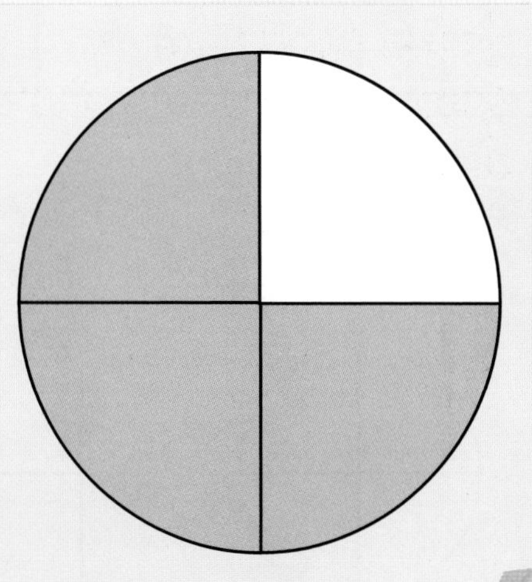

Lesson 6: **Equal fractions**

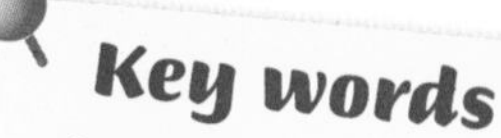

- Recognise that $\frac{1}{2}$ and $\frac{2}{4}$ are the same

Key words
- half
- halves
- quarters
- equal

Number

Discover

There is half an apple on one plate and two quarters of an apple on the other plate.

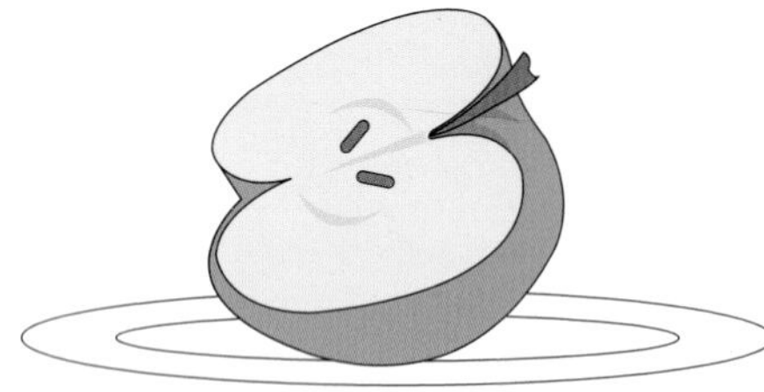

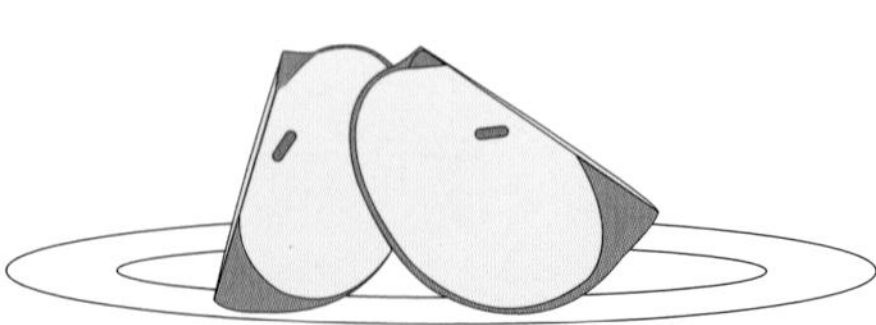

Learn

One half is the same amount as two quarters.

1			
$\frac{1}{2}$		$\frac{1}{2}$	
$\frac{1}{4}$	$\frac{1}{4}$	$\frac{1}{4}$	$\frac{1}{4}$

Example

Tick the shapes that have an equal fraction shaded.

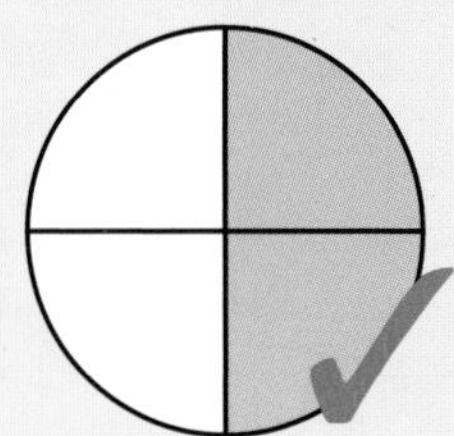

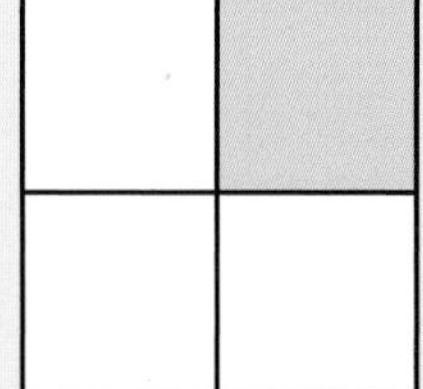

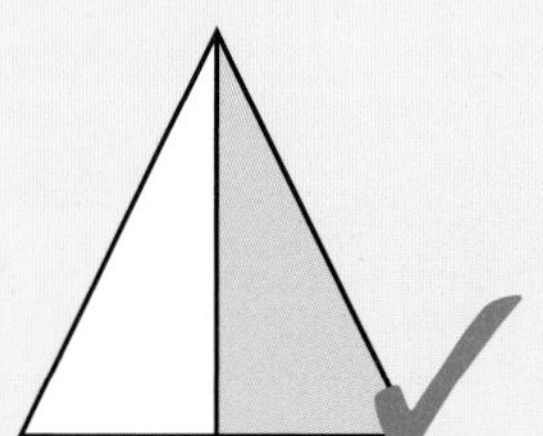

Lesson 7: **Halves of numbers of objects**

- Find halves of small numbers of objects

Key words
- half
- halves
- share
- divide
- equal

Discover

Half of these 6 melons will fit in each bag. That's 3 melons in each bag.

Learn

To halve an amount, you share it between 2.

8

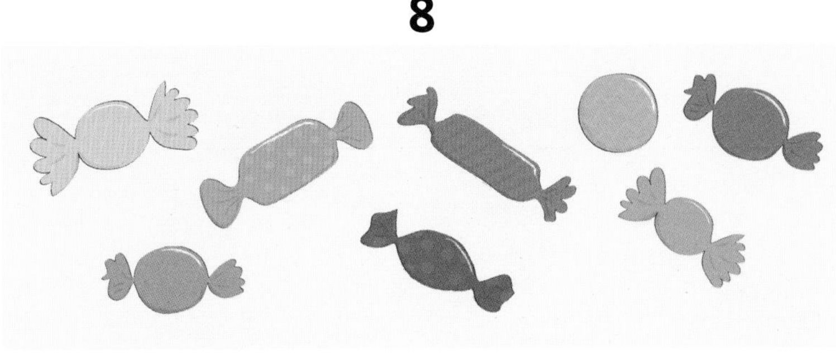

4

4

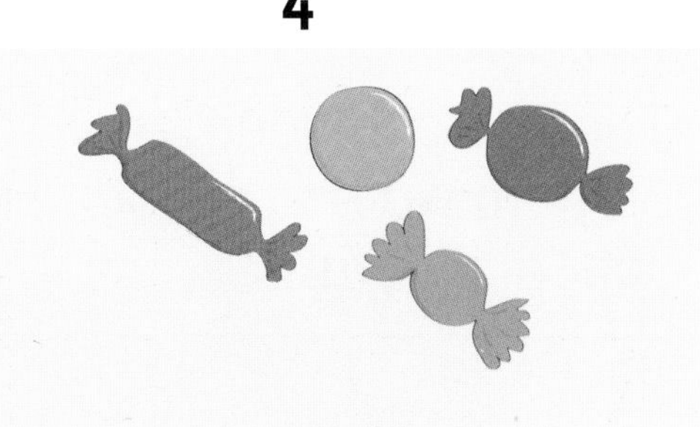

Half of 8 is 4.

Lesson 8: **Quarters of numbers of objects**

- Find one quarter of small numbers of objects

Key words
- quarters
- share
- divide
- equal

Discover

There are 12 strawberries on the cake.
How many are there on each quarter?

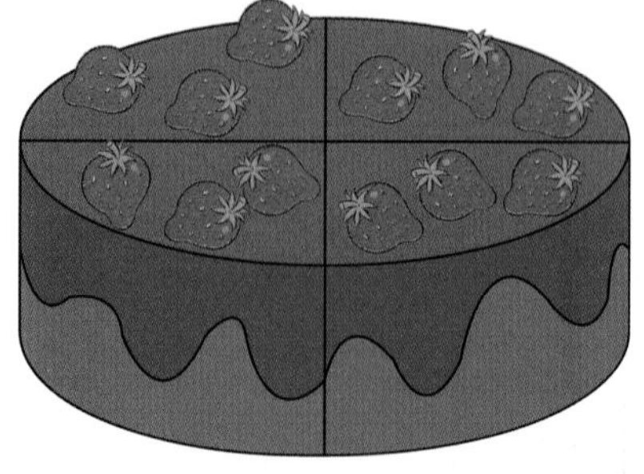

Learn

To find quarters of an amount, you share it between 4.

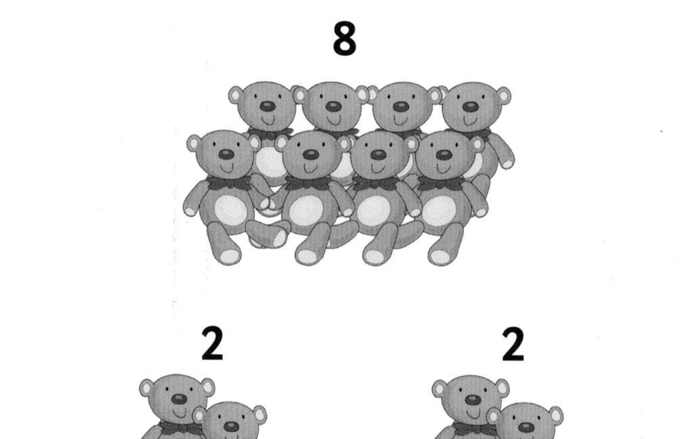

One quarter of 8 is 2.

Example

There are 16 learners in the class. One quarter of them walk to school. How many walk to school in total?

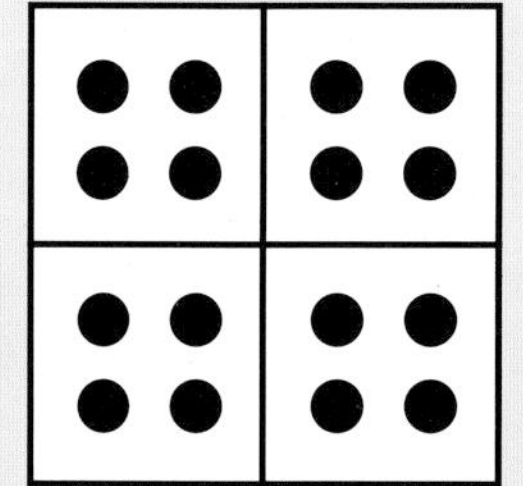

Lesson 1: Number pairs for 10 and 20

- Know all the number pairs for 10 and 20

Key words
- number bonds
- number pairs
- add
- total
- equals

Discover

Number pairs for 10 are numbers that add to make 10.

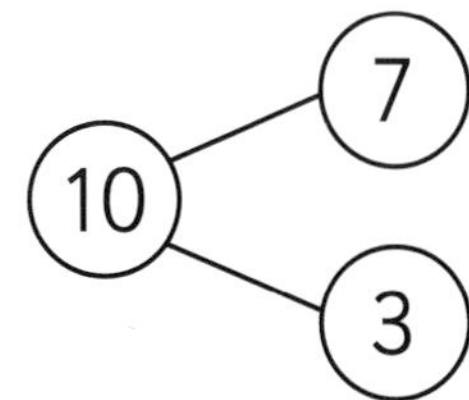

Number pairs for 20 are numbers that add to make 20.

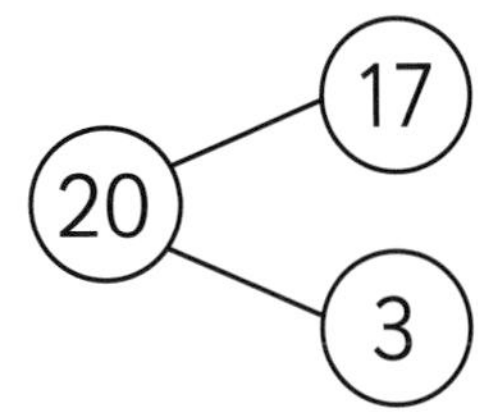

Learn

These pairs of numbers make 10 when you add them together.

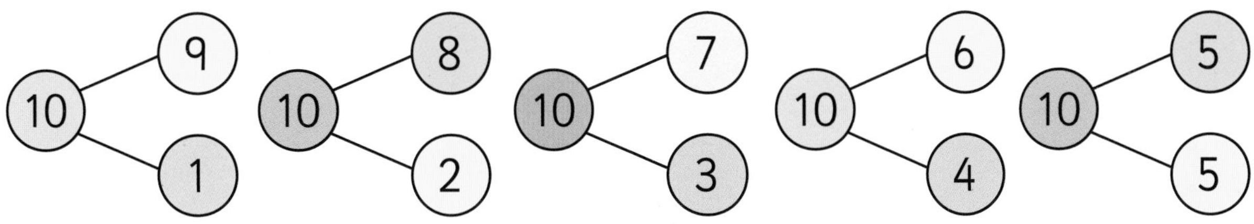

To find number bonds for 20, add 10 to one of the numbers.

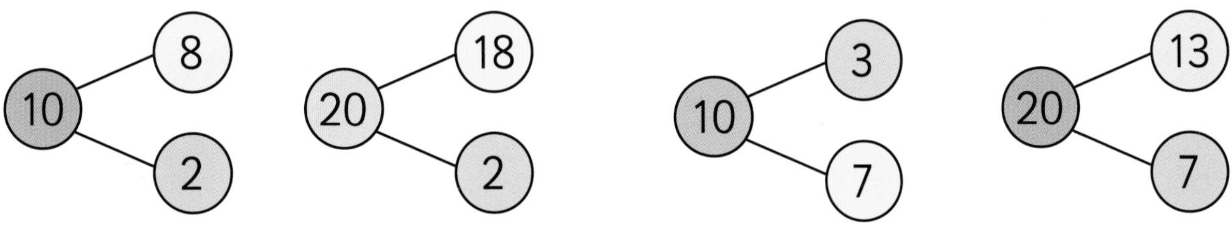

Lesson 2: Addition and subtraction bonds to 20 (1)

- Find number bonds for a number from 10 to 20
- Write number sentences to match these number bonds

Key words
- number bonds
- number pairs
- add
- subtract
- take away

Discover

There are many different ways to make a number.

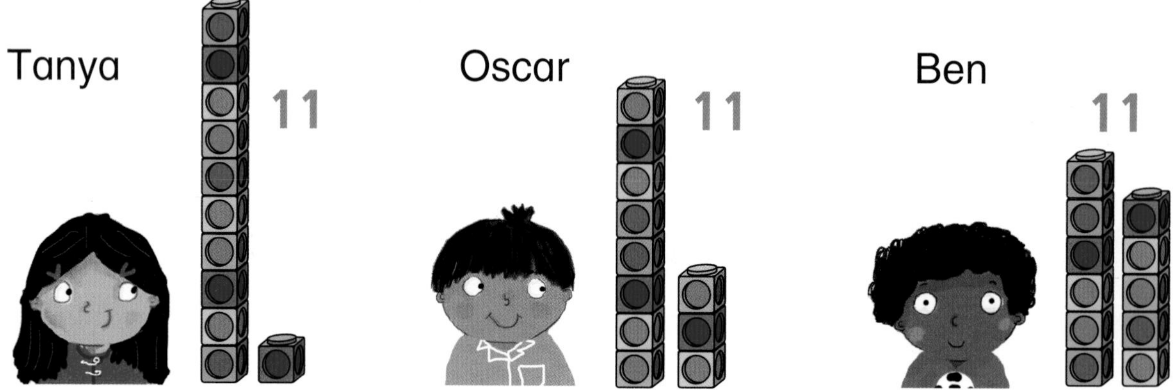

Learn

These are the number bonds for 13.

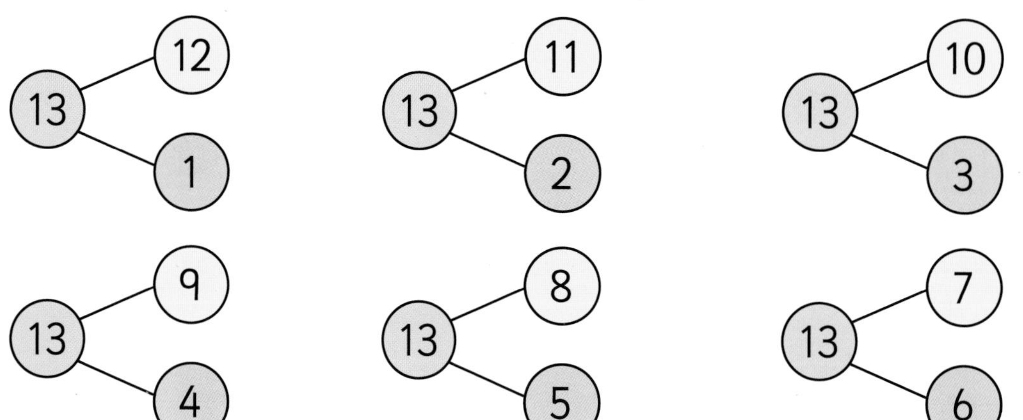

Example

You can write number sentences to match a number bond.

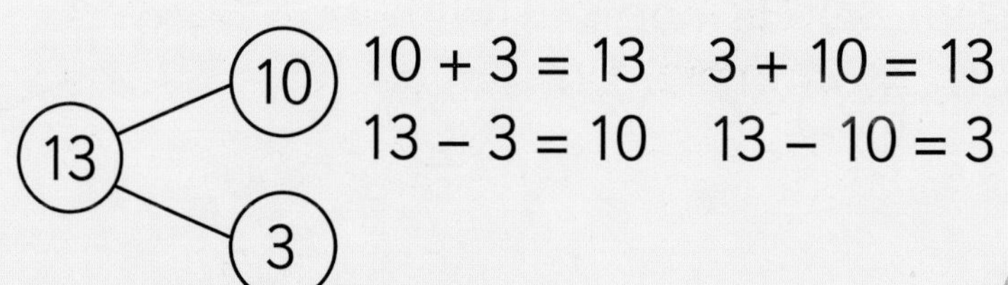

$10 + 3 = 13$ $3 + 10 = 13$

$13 - 3 = 10$ $13 - 10 = 3$

Lesson 3: **Multiples of 10 with a total of 100**

- Find pairs of multiples of 10 that make 100

Key words

- tens
- number bonds
- number pairs
- add
- subtract

Discover

Number bonds for 10 can help you find number bonds for 100.

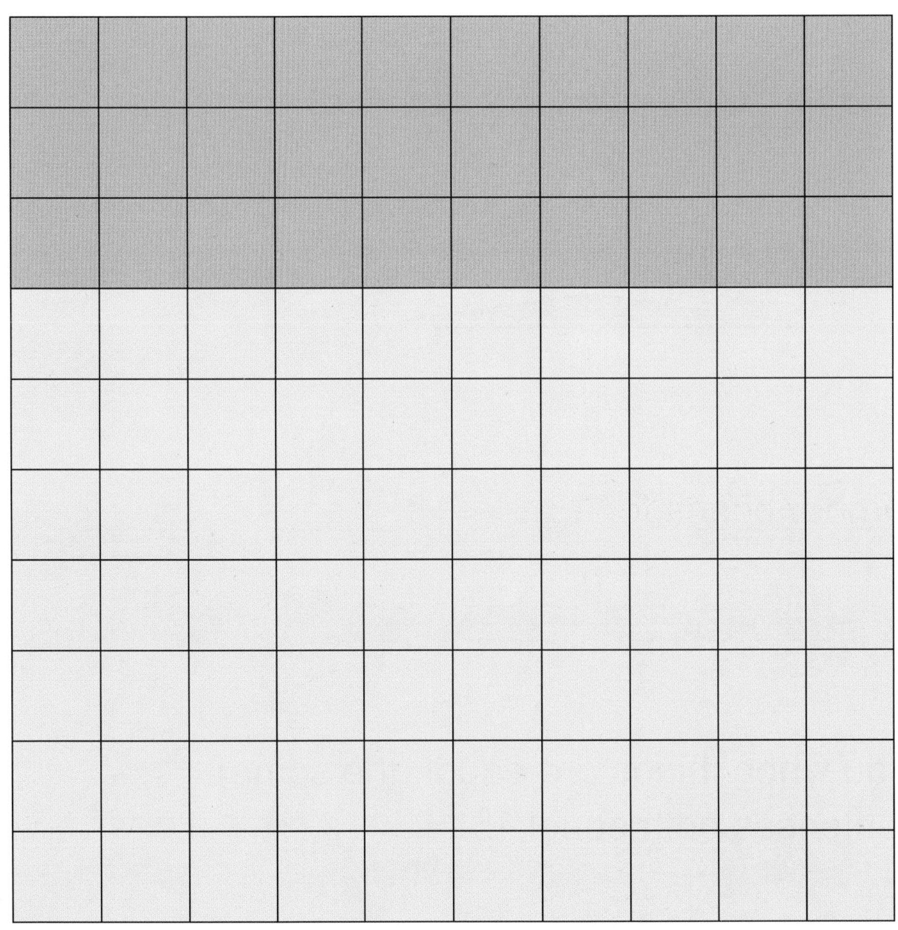

30

70

Learn

Number bonds for 100 follow the same pattern as number bonds for 10.

7 + 3 = 10   70 + 30 = 100

5 + 5 = 10   50 + 50 = 100

Lesson 4: The equals sign (=)

- Use the = sign to show that two number statements are equal

Key words
- equal
- equals
- the same as

Discover

Different number sentences can equal the same amount.

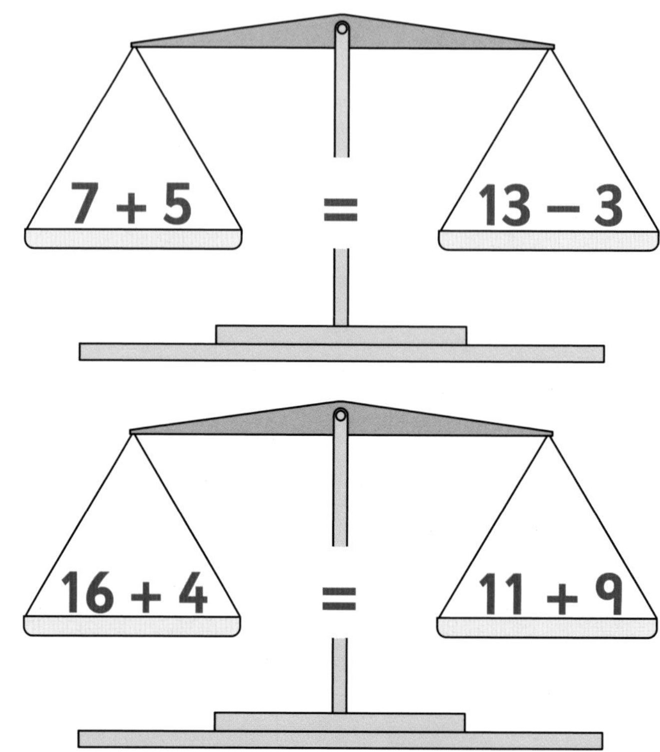

Learn

The = sign tells you when things are equal (the same).
These number sentences both equal 15, so they are equal.

$$8 + 7 = 20 - 5$$

Example

Write a number sentence to make this statement true.

$13 + 2 = 20 - 5$

Lesson 5: **Adding more than two numbers**

- Add more than two small numbers together

Key words
- add
- plus
- count on
- number line

Number

Discover

Sometimes you need to add more than two numbers together.

Learn

To add more than two numbers, it can help to order them from largest to smallest.

3 + 6 + 1 + 2 ➔ 6 + 3 + 2 + 1

Find the largest number on your number line, then count on each of the other numbers.

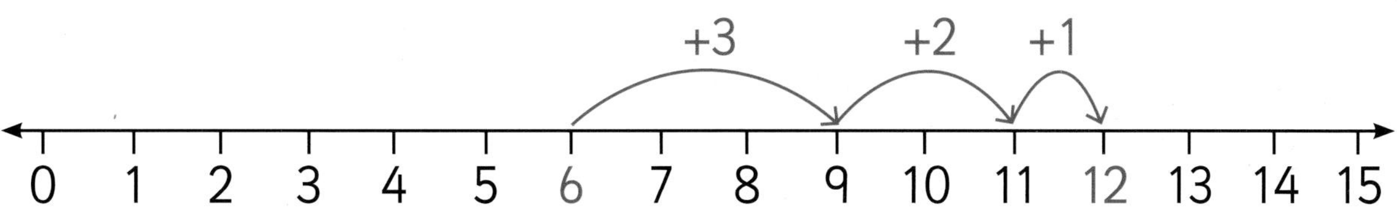

Lesson 6: **Adding a single-digit number to a 2-digit number (1)**

- Add a single digit to a 2-digit number by counting on

Key words
- add
- plus
- count on
- digits

Discover

45 + 3 = ?

Counting on from a larger number is easier than counting on from a smaller number.

Learn

To add a 2-digit number to a single-digit number, start with the larger number and count on.

Hold up your fingers as you count until they match the smaller number.

62 + 6 = ?

62 + 6 = 68

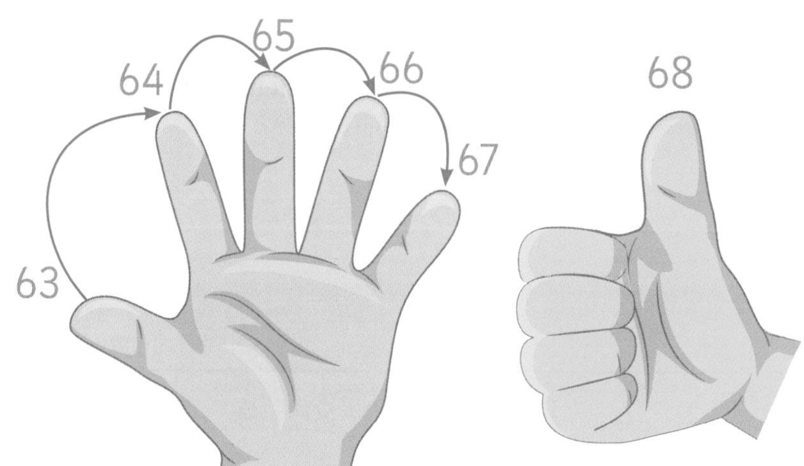

Lesson 7: **Subtracting a single-digit number from a 2-digit number (1)**

- Subtract a single digit from a 2-digit number by counting back

Key words
- subtract
- take away
- count back
- digits

Number

Discover

Non has 15 one cent coins. Three of them are taken away. She has 12 left.

Learn

To subtract a single-digit number from a 2-digit number, start with the larger number and count back.

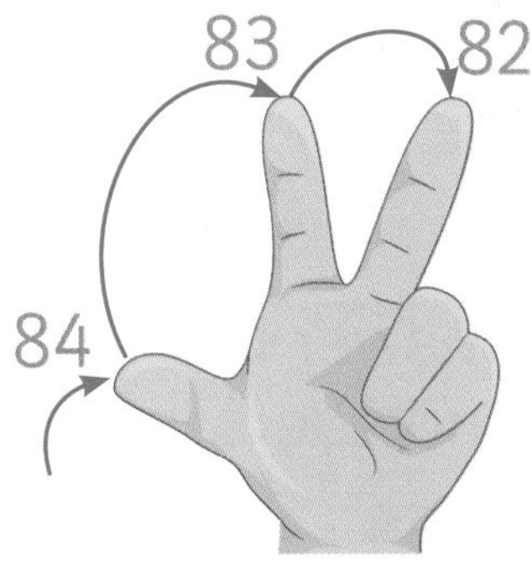

85 – 3 = 82

Hold up your fingers as you count until they match the smaller number.

85 – 3 = ?

Tip! Hold your fingers...

Lesson 8: **In any order?**

- Understand that addition can be done in any order but that subtraction cannot

Key words
- add
- plus
- subtract
- take away

Discover

You can add numbers in any order.

7 + 3 + 1 = 11

1 + 7 + 3 = 11

3 + 1 + 7 = 11

But you cannot subtract numbers in any order.
The answer to **9 – 3** is not the same as the answer to **3 – 9**.

Learn

Check an answer to an addition by adding the numbers in a different order.

6 + 8 = **14** → 8 + 6 = **14**

Check an answer to a subtraction by adding the answer to the smaller number.

12 – 4 = **8**  8 + 4 = **12**

Lesson 1: **Addition and subtraction bonds to 20 (2)**

- Find number bonds for numbers to 20 and write additions and subtractions to match

Key words

- number bonds
- number pairs
- add
- subtract

Discover

There are many pairs of numbers that add together to make 14.
Here are four of them.

12 + 2 = 14	7 + 7 = 14
8 + 6 = 14	10 + 4 = 14

Learn

You can write four different number sentences to match a number bond.

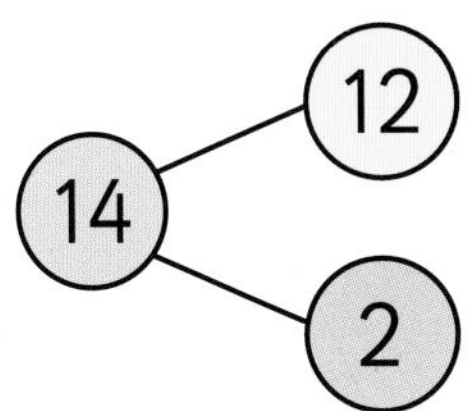

12 + 2 = 14	2 + 12 = 14
14 − 2 = 12	14 − 12 = 2

Example

Write a pair of numbers that total 17. [9] and [8]

Now write one addition and one subtraction to match it.

[9] + [8] = 17

17 − [9] = [8]

Lesson 2: Adding tens to a 2-digit number

- Add multiples of 10 to a 2-digit number

Key words
- tens
- multiples
- add
- plus
- more
- count on

Discover

How could Tom use a 100 square to work out the answer?

1	2	3	4	5	6	7	8	9	10
11	12	13	14	15	16	17	18	19	20
21	22	23	24	25	26	27	28	29	30
31	32	33	34	35	36	37	38	39	40
41	42	43	44	45	46	47	48	49	50
51	52	53	54	55	56	57	58	59	60
61	62	63	64	65	66	67	68	69	70
71	72	73	74	75	76	77	78	79	80
81	82	83	84	85	86	87	88	89	90
91	92	93	94	95	96	97	98	99	100

Learn

To add multiples of 10 to a number, find the number on the 100 square and count on in tens by moving down the 100 square.

13 + 20 = 33

1	2	3	4	5	6	7	8	9	10
11	12	13	14	15	16	17	18	19	20
21	22	23	24	25	26	27	28	29	30
31	32	33	34	35	36	37	38	39	40

Lesson 3: **Adding a single-digit number to a 2-digit number (2)**

- Add a single-digit number to a 2-digit number

Key words
- digits
- add
- plus
- count on

Discover

How many potatoes altogether?

52

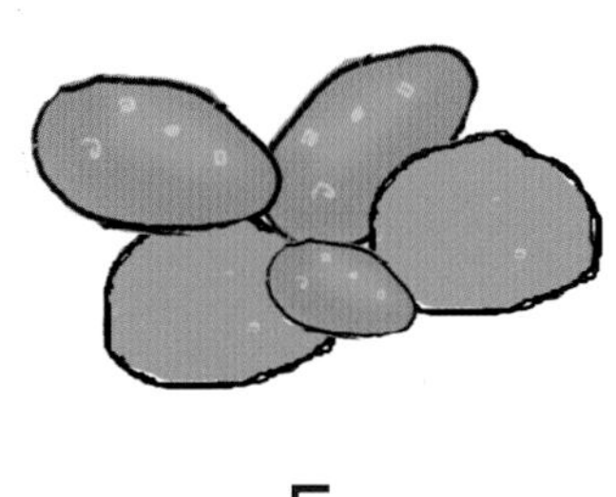

5

Learn

To add a single-digit number to a 2-digit number, find the 2-digit number on a 100 square and count on.

24 + 3 = ?

21	22	23	(24)	25	26	(27)	28	29	30

24 + 3 = **27**

Example

Write the number sentence and solve the addition.

What is 31 + 7?

30	(31)	32	33	34	35	36	37	(38)	39	40

31 + 7 = 38

Lesson 4: **Adding pairs of 2-digit numbers (1)**

- Use partitioning to add pairs of 2-digit numbers

Key words

- add
- plus
- partitioning
- tens
- ones

Discover

64 + 15 = ?

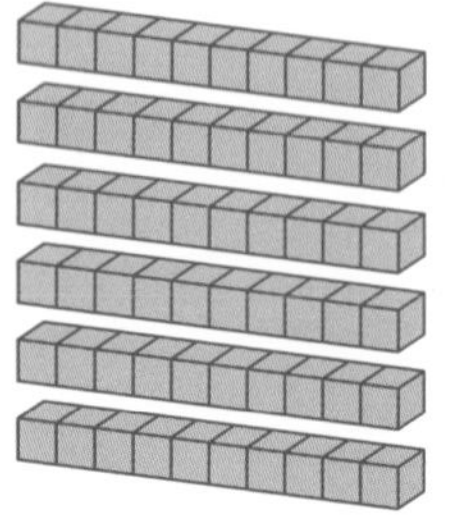

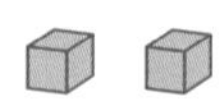

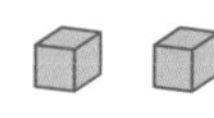

+

Learn

To work out 36 + 23, use Base 10 to partition both numbers into tens and ones.

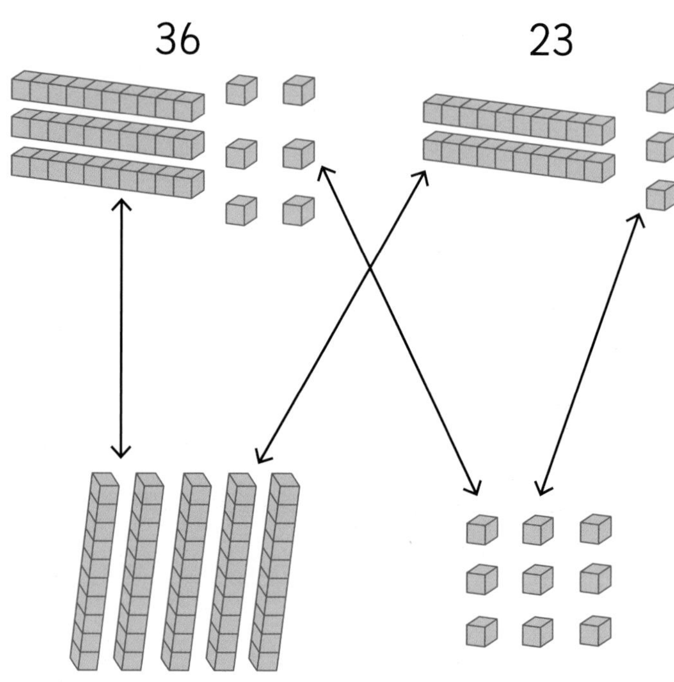

Add the tens together, and add the ones together.

Then add the ones to the tens.

So, 36 + 23 = 59

50 + 9 = 59

Lesson 5: 'Take away' and 'difference'

- Solve a subtraction by taking away or finding the difference

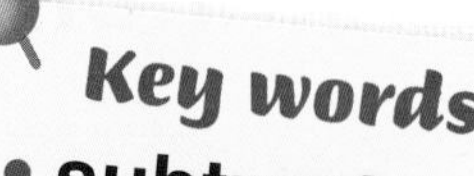

Key words
- subtract
- take away
- difference

Number

Discover

The children are solving the subtraction in different ways.

Learn

10 – 3 =

To **take away**, start on 10 and count back 3.

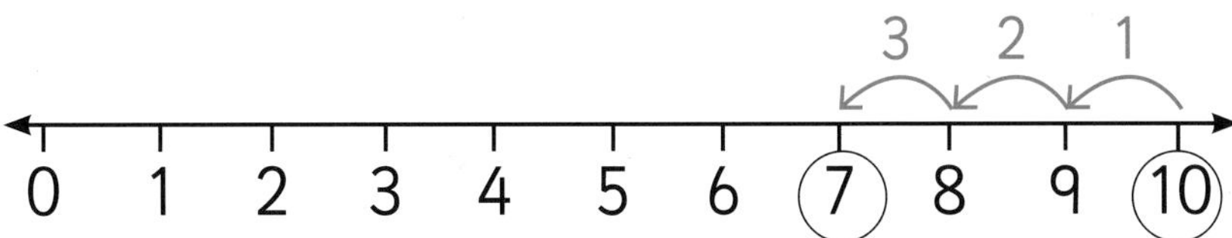

To **find the difference** between 10 and 3, start on 3 and make a jump for each number on the number line until you reach 10. Count the jumps to find the answer.

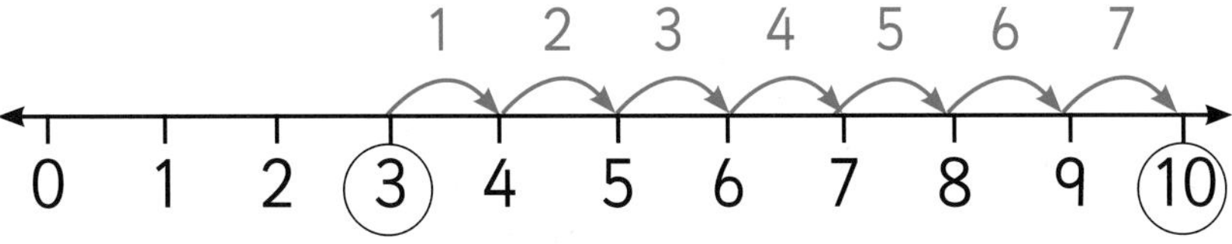

Lesson 6: Subtracting tens from a 2-digit number

- Subtract multiples of 10 from a 2-digit number

Key words
- subtract
- take away
- tens
- multiples

Discover

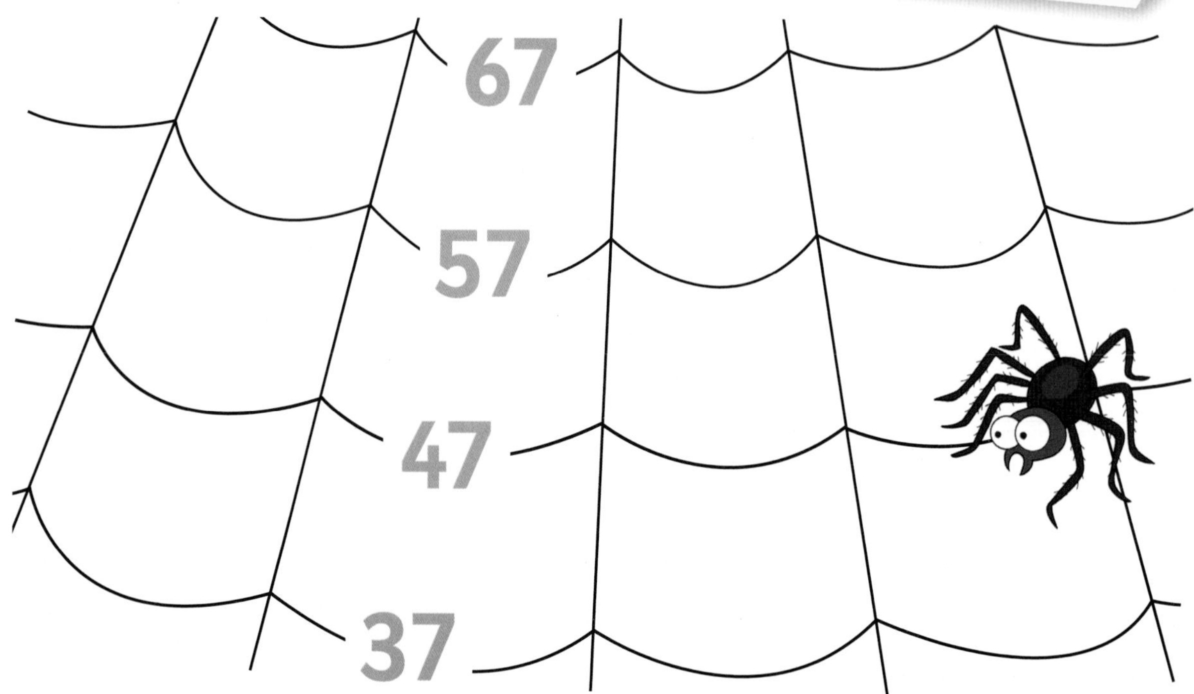

You can count back in tens from any number.

Learn

To subtract multiples of 10 from a number, count back in tens.

94 – 30 = 64

51	52	53	54	55	56	57	58	59	60
61	62	63	64	65	66	67	68	69	70
71	72	73	74	75	76	77	78	79	80
81	82	83	84	85	86	87	88	89	90
91	92	93	94	95	96	97	98	99	100

Lesson 7: **Subtracting a single-digit number from a 2-digit number (2)**

- Subtract a single-digit number from a 2-digit number

Key words
- subtract
- take away
- count back
- digits

Discover

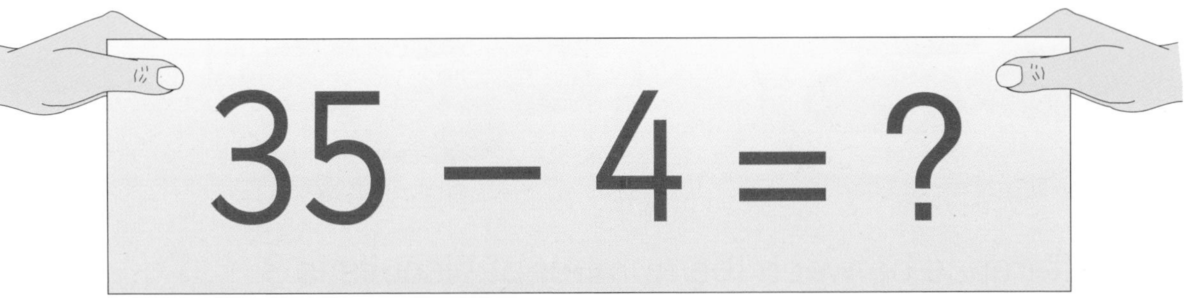

How would you work out the answer?

Learn

To subtract a single-digit number from a 2-digit number, first find the larger number on the 100 square.

Then, count back the number of squares shown by the single-digit number.

38 – 5 = ?

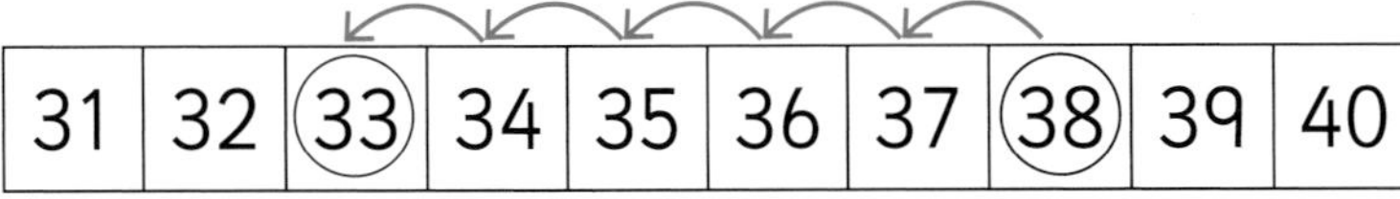

31	32	(33)	34	35	36	37	(38)	39	40

38 – 5 = 33

Lesson 8: **Finding the difference (1)**

- Find the difference between two numbers

Key words

- **subtract**
- **difference**

Discover

The difference between the number of biscuits is 3.

Learn

To find the difference between two numbers, first find the smaller number on a number line.

Then, count the number of jumps you make until you reach the larger number.

The difference between 25 and 28 is **3**.

Example

Count the number of jumps to find the difference between these numbers.

54 and 57 [3]

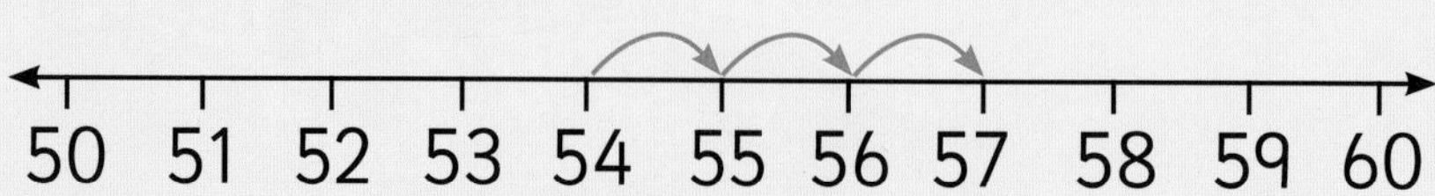

Lesson 1: **Addition and subtraction**

- Find number bonds for numbers to 20 and write additions and subtractions to match

Key words
- number bonds
- number pairs
- add
- subtract

Discover

Which pairs of numbers when added or subtracted make 15?

8 + 7   19 – 4   17 – 2   13 + 2

Learn

You can add different pairs of numbers to make the same number.

Addition

$6 + 6 = 12$ $10 + 2 = 12$ $4 + 8 = 12$ $7 + 5 = 12$

Subtraction

$12 - 6 = 6$ $12 - 2 = 10$ $12 - 8 = 4$ $12 - 5 = 7$

Example

Write a pair of numbers that make 12.

[7] + [5] = 12

Now use the same numbers in a subtraction.

12 – [5] = [7]

Lesson 2: Adding and subtracting tens to and from a 2-digit number

- Add and subtract multiples of 10 to and from a 2-digit number

Key words

- tens
- multiples
- add
- plus
- more
- count on

Discover

1	2	3	4	5	6	7	8	9	10
11	12	13	14	15	16	17	18	19	20
21	22	23	24	25	26	27	28	29	30
31	32	33	34	35	36	37	38	39	40
41	42	43	44	45	46	47	48	49	50
51	52	53	54	55	56	57	58	59	60
61	62	63	64	65	66	67	68	69	70
71	72	73	74	75	76	77	78	79	80
81	82	83	84	85	86	87	88	89	90
91	92	93	94	95	96	97	98	99	100

Count the tens to find what has been added to 14 to make 64.

Learn

To add a multiple of 10 to a number, count on in tens. **61 + 30 = 91**

61	62	63	64	65	66	67	68	69	70
71	72	73	74	75	76	77	78	79	80
81	82	83	84	85	86	87	88	89	90
91	92	93	94	95	96	97	98	99	100

To subtract a multiple of 10 from a number, count back in tens. **84 – 20 = 64**

61	62	63	64	65	66	67	68	69	70
71	72	73	74	75	76	77	78	79	80
81	82	83	84	85	86	87	88	89	90

Lesson 3: **Adding and subtracting single-digit numbers**

- Add and subtract a single-digit number to and from a 2-digit number

Key words
- add
- plus
- subtract
- take away
- count on
- count back

Discover

11 + 8   25 + 9   29 – 3   44 – 7

How would you work out the answers?

Learn

Use number facts that you know to help.

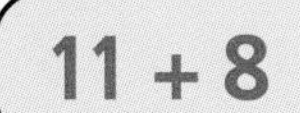

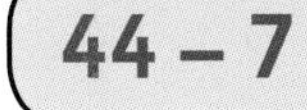

25 + 9

29 – 3

Lesson 4: Adding pairs of 2-digit numbers (2)

- Add a pair of 2-digit numbers together by partitioning

- add
- plus
- partitioning
- tens
- ones

Number

Discover

How could partitioning help you to add these numbers?

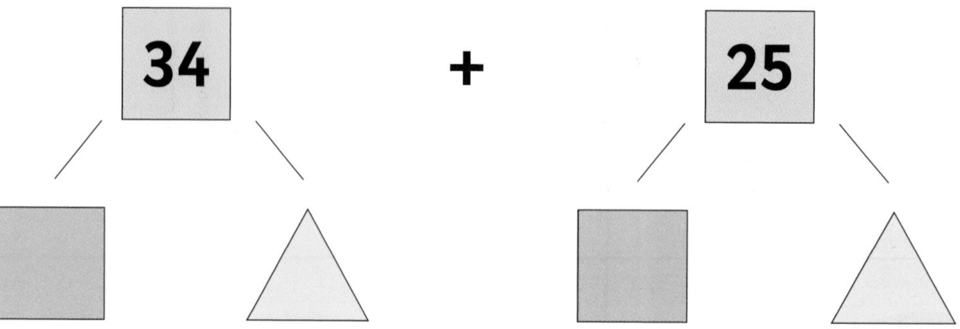

Learn

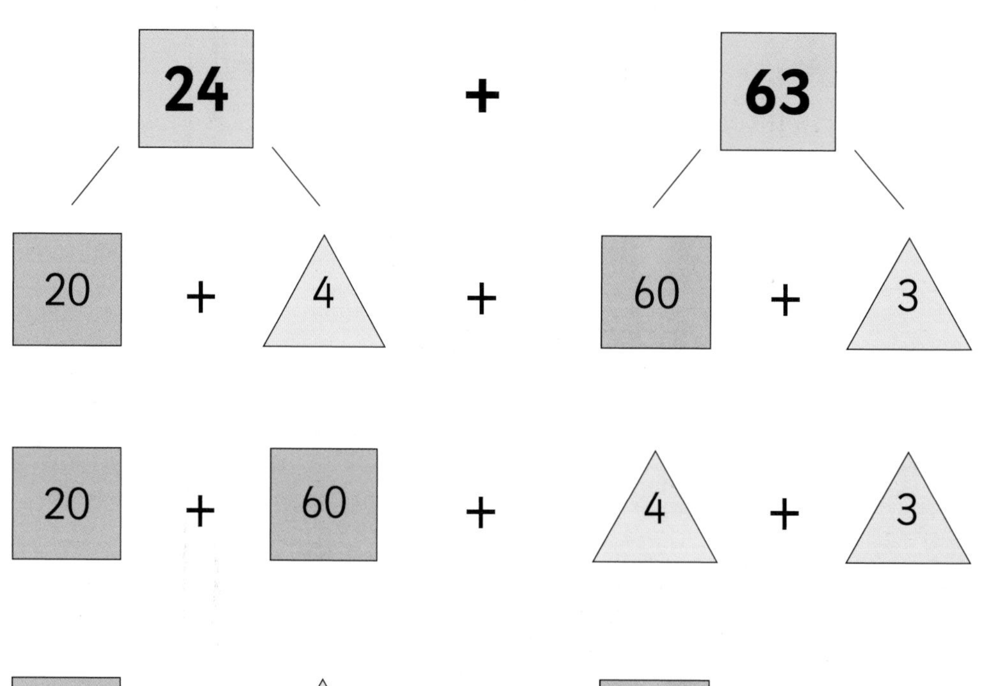

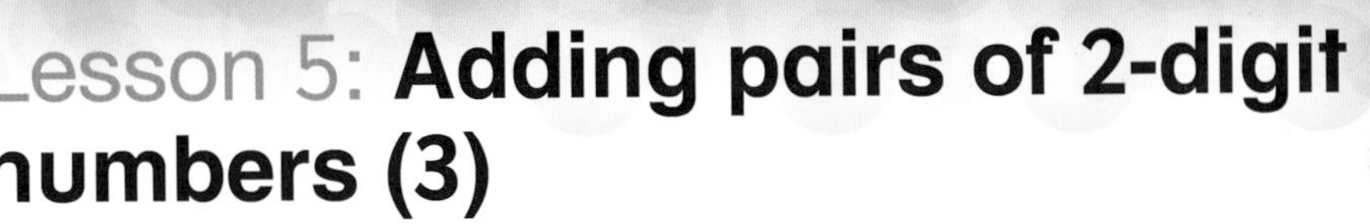

Lesson 5: **Adding pairs of 2-digit numbers (3)**

- Use partitioning to add pairs of 2-digit numbers

Key words
- **add**
- **plus**
- **partitioning**
- **tens**
- **ones**

Discover

Partitioning 2-digit numbers, then adding the tens and ones helps you to add them together.

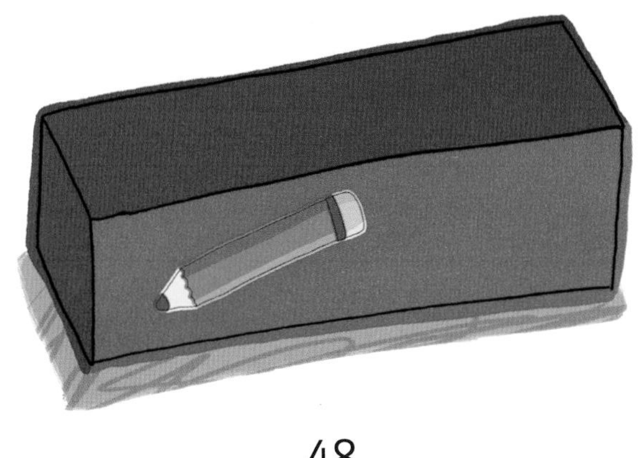

48

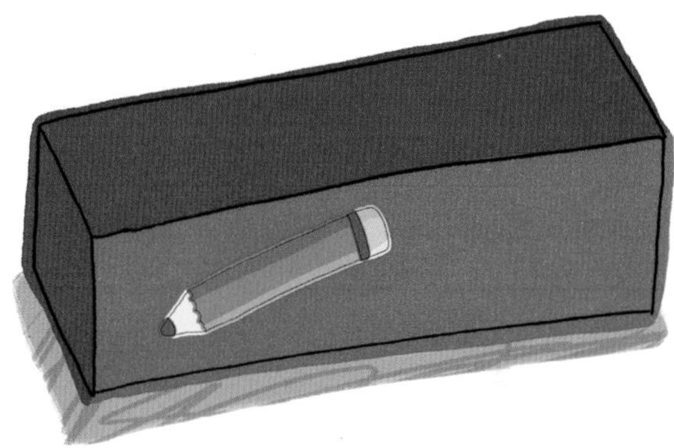

24

Learn

Partition the smaller number, then add the tens and ones to the larger number.

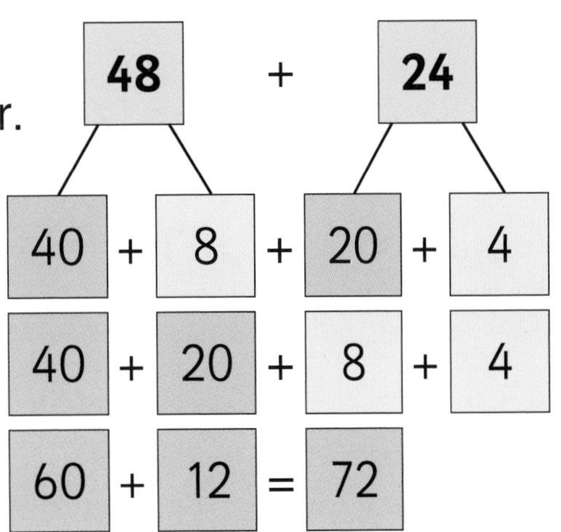

48 + 24 = 48 + 20 + 4

= 68 + 4

= 72

Example

56 + 36 = 56 + 30 + 6

= 86 + 6

= 92

Lesson 6: **Missing number problems (addition)**

- Find the missing number in an addition number sentence

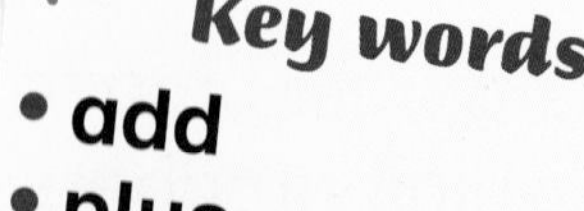

Key words

- **add**
- **plus**
- **equals**
- **number bonds**

Discover

How many more eggs does Leroy need?

Learn

Find the missing number by counting on until you reach the answer.

13 + ☐ = 19

1 2 3 4 5 6

11	12	(13)	14	15	16	17	18	(19)	20

Count on from 13 to 19 to find how many more to make 19.

13 + 6 = 19

Example

48 + 8 = 56

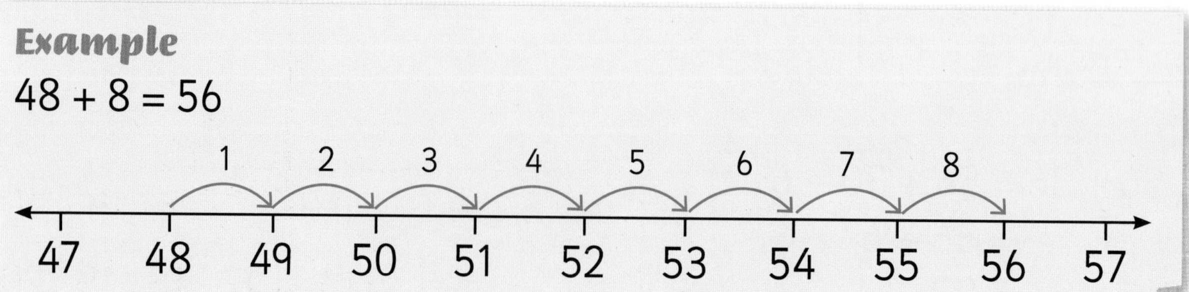

Lesson 7: **Missing number problems (subtraction)**

- Find the missing number in a subtraction number sentence

Key words
- subtract
- take away
- equals

Discover

How many cakes has Sammy eaten?

Learn

To find the missing number, count on from the answer to the first number to find the difference.

20 – ☐ = 14 → 20 – 6 = 14

11	12	13	(14)	15	16	17	18	19	(20)

To find the missing number, add the given number to the answer.

☐ – 2 = 7 → 9 – 2 = 7

1	2	3	4	5	6	(7)	8	(9)	10
11	12	13	14	15	16	17	18	19	20

Lesson 8: **Finding the difference (2)**

Number

- Find the difference between two numbers

Key words
- subtract
- difference

Discover

You can count on from 25 to 28 to find the difference between the ages.

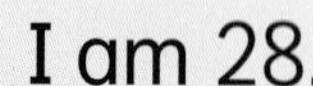

Learn

You can use a number line to find the difference between 63 and 68.

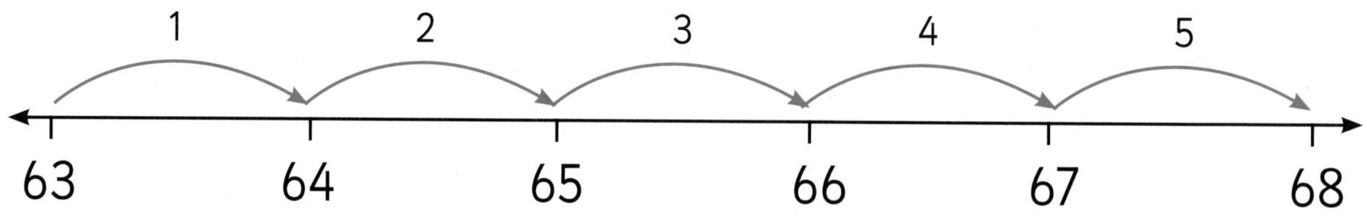

Count the number of jumps. The number of jumps you have counted at the end is the answer.

Lesson 1: Multiplying numbers

- Use the × sign
- Understand multiplication as an array

Key words
- multiply
- times
- groups of
- lots of
- array

Discover

An **array** can show a multiplication.

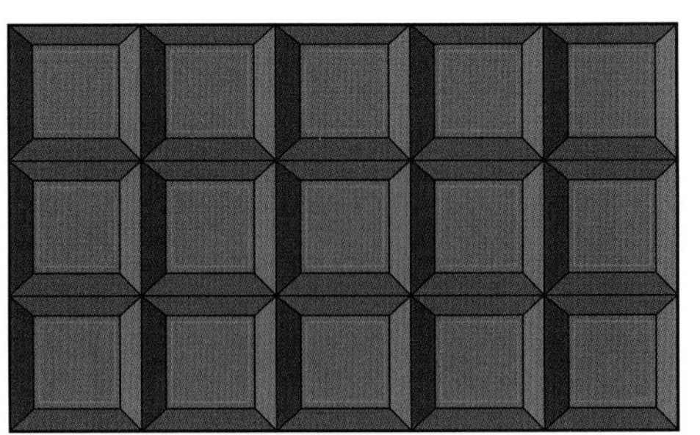

3×5

Learn

You can solve multiplications by making an array.

If you swap the numbers around, the answer is the same.

$5 \times 2 = 10$ $2 \times 5 = 10$

Example

Draw an array of dots to match the number sentence. Count the dots to find the answer.

$2 \times 7 =$ 14

Lesson 2: **The 2 times table**

- Recognise multiples of 2
- Use an array to recall 2 times table facts

- twos
- multiples
- multiply
- times
- lots of
- array

Discover

How many children? How many flags does each child have? How many flags altogether?

Learn

The **multiples** of 2 are the numbers you say when you count on from zero in 2s.

1	2	3	4	5	6	7	8	9	10
2	4	6	8	10	12	14	16	18	20

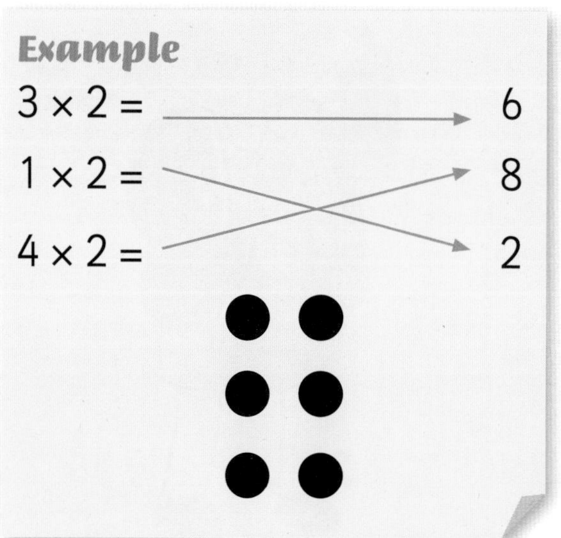

Lesson 3: **The 5 times table**

- Recognise multiples of 5
- Use an array to recall 5 times table facts

Key words
- fives
- multiples
- multiply
- times
- lots of
- array

Discover

How many pots? How many crayons in each pot? How many crayons altogether?

Learn

The **multiples** of 5 are the numbers you say when you count on from zero in 5s.

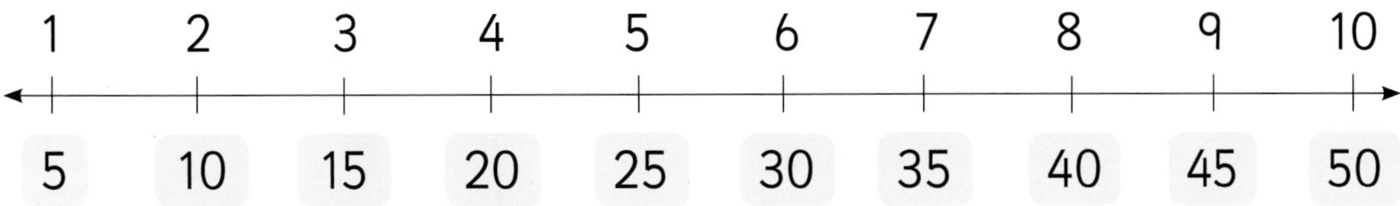

Example

Draw an array on your mini whiteboard to show this 5 times table fact. Then write the answer.

$2 \times 5 =$ 10

● ● ● ● ●
● ● ● ● ●

Lesson 4: The 10 times table

- Recognise multiples of 10
- Use an array to recall 10 times table facts

Key words
- tens
- multiples
- multiply
- times
- lots of
- array

Discover

How many socks? How many spots on each sock? How many spots altogether?

Learn

The multiples of 10 are the numbers you say when you count in 10s from 0.

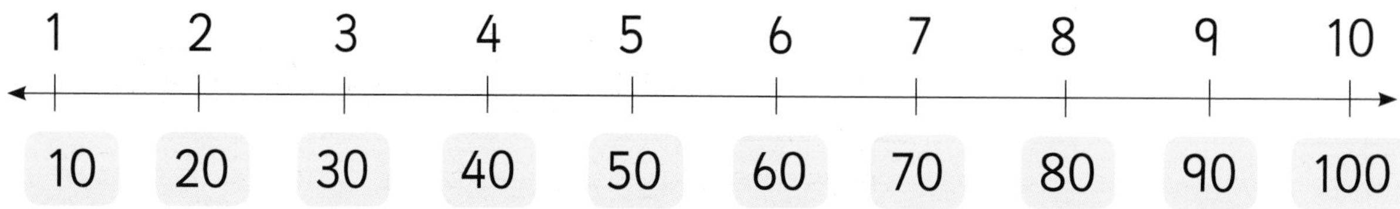

Example

Draw an array on your mini whiteboard to show this 10 times table fact.
Write the answer.

3 × 10 = 30

Lesson 1: Doubles (1)

- Find doubles

Key words
- multiply
- times
- double

Discover

If you have double, you have twice as many.

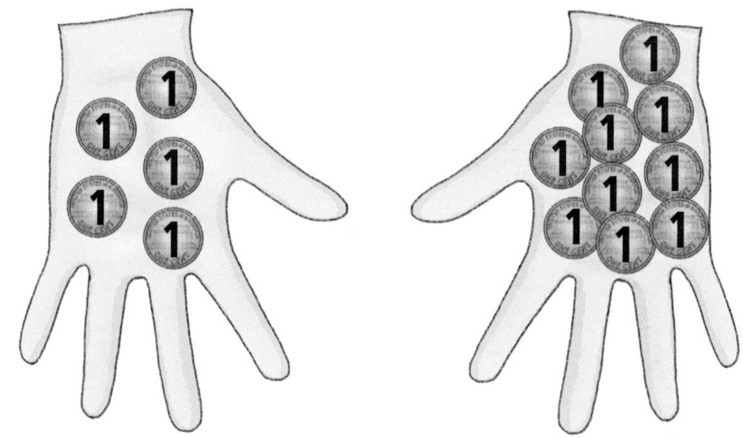

Learn

To double a number on a 100 square, start from your number and count on by the same number.

1	2	3	4	5	6	7	8	9	10
11	12	13	14	15	16	17	18	19	20
21	22	23	24	25	26	27	28	29	30
31	32	33	34	35	36	37	38	39	40
41	42	43	44	45	46	47	48	49	50

Doubling is the same as multiplying by 2.

Double 7 is 14.

$7 \times 2 = 14$

Example

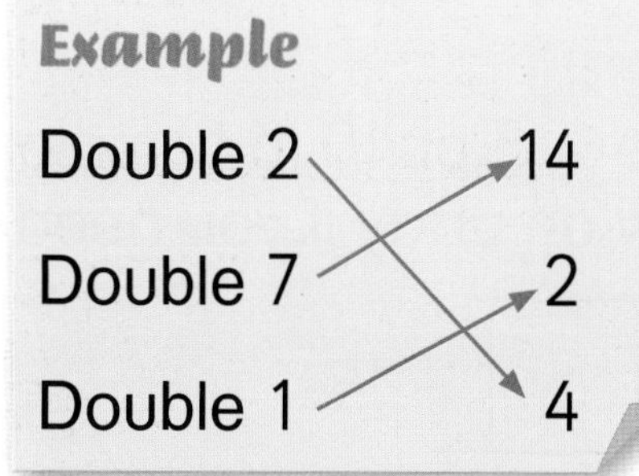

Lesson 2: **2s, 5s and 10s (1)**

- Recognise multiples of 2, 5 and 10
- Use an array to recall 2, 5 and 10 times tables facts

Key words
- multiples
- multiply
- times
- lots of
- array

Discover

Being able to skip-count from 0 in 2s, 5s and 10s helps in multiplication.

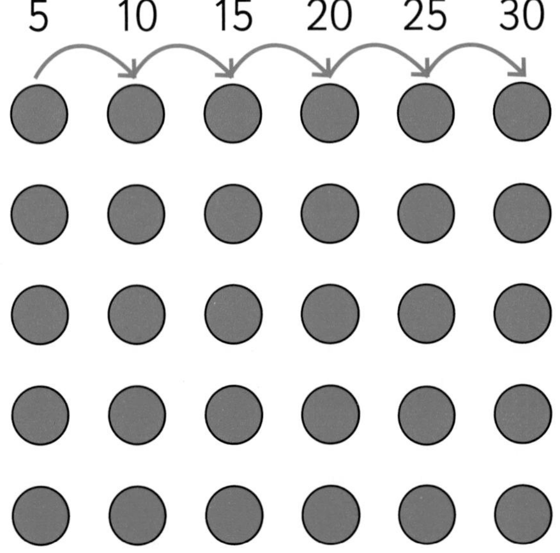

Learn

Multiples of 2 are even numbers.
They end in 0, 2, 4, 6 or 8.

Multiples of 5 end in 5 or 0.

Multiples of 10 end in 0.

Example

Write 2, 5 or 10 to complete the times table fact.
Draw an array if you need to.

3 × [5] = 15

Lesson 3: **2s, 5s and 10s (2)**

• Use repeated addition to multiply

Key words
- multiples
- multiply
- times
- lots of
- array

Discover

3 + 3 + 3 + 3 = 12

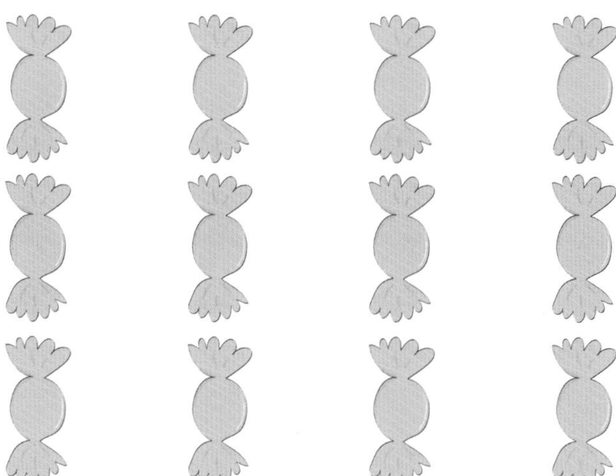

Learn

Multiplication is really just repeated addition. The × symbol can be read as 'times'. So 3 × 4 means 'add the number 4 three times'.

4 + 4 + 4 is the same as 3 × 4
or

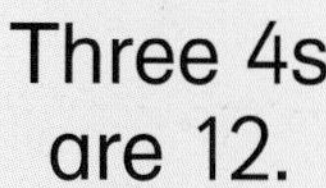

Lesson 4: **Adding groups**

- Count in groups of 2s, 5s or 10s to solve multiplication problems

Key words

- multiply
- times
- groups
- add
- count on

Discover

2 + 2 + 2 + 2 + 2 + 2 is the same as 2 × 6

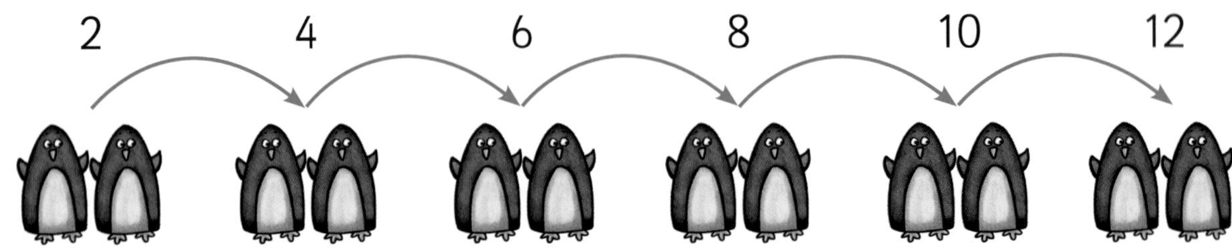

Learn

Add groups of amounts to multiply.
Skip-counting using a number line or 100 square can help.

3 × 4 is the same as 3 + 3 + 3 + 3

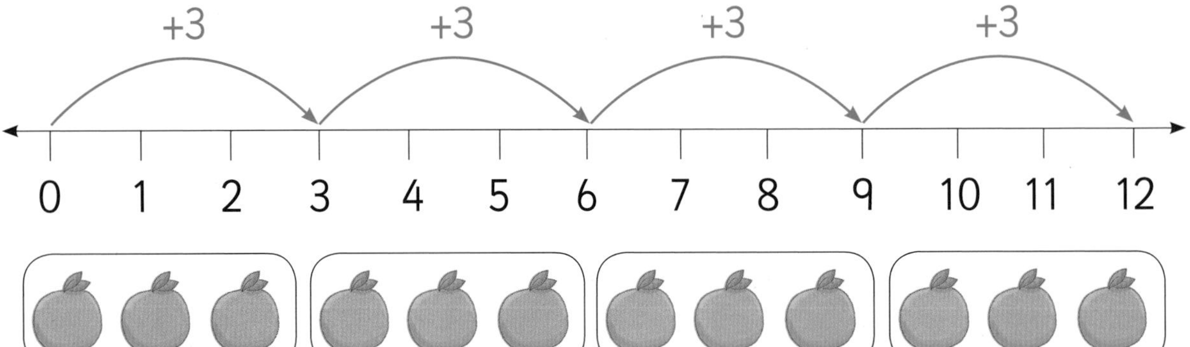

Example

Find the answer to 3 × 5.

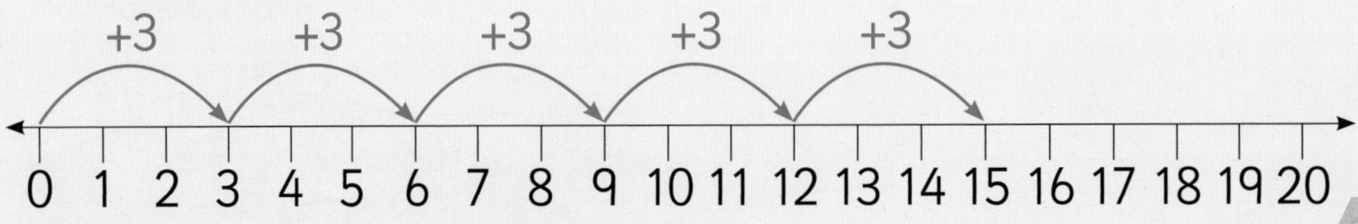

Lesson 5: **Making groups**

- Make groups to solve division problems
- Use the ÷ sign

Key words
- divide
- share
- groups

Discover

You can divide amounts by sharing them into groups.

Learn

$8 \div 2$ is a division problem. We need to find out how many groups of 2 there are in 8.

- The first number tells you how many you have to share.
- The second number tells you how many in each group.

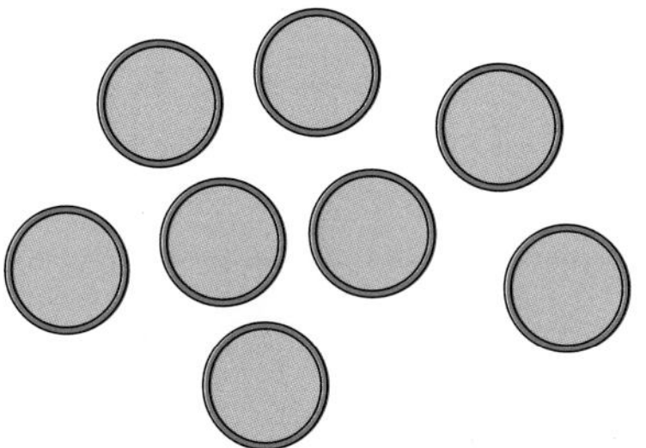

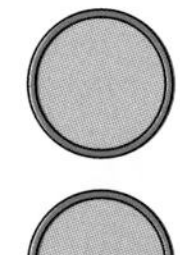

$8 \div 2 = 4$

Example

Use grouping to find out how many groups of 5 there are in 10.

$10 \div 5 =$ 2

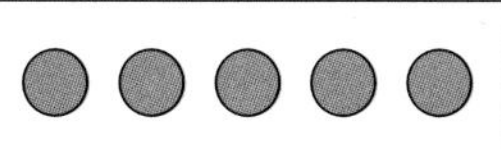
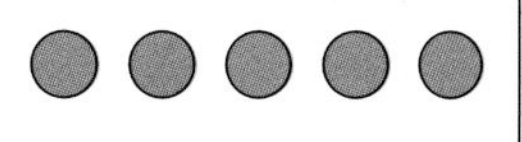

Lesson 6: Dividing between 2, 5 and 10

- Know division facts for 2, 5 and 10

Key words
- divide
- division
- share

Discover

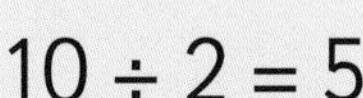

Learn

To work out a division, you can use step-counting.

To work out 20 ÷ 5, count in 5s until you reach 20.

The answer is the number of 5s that you counted.

20 ÷ 5 = 4

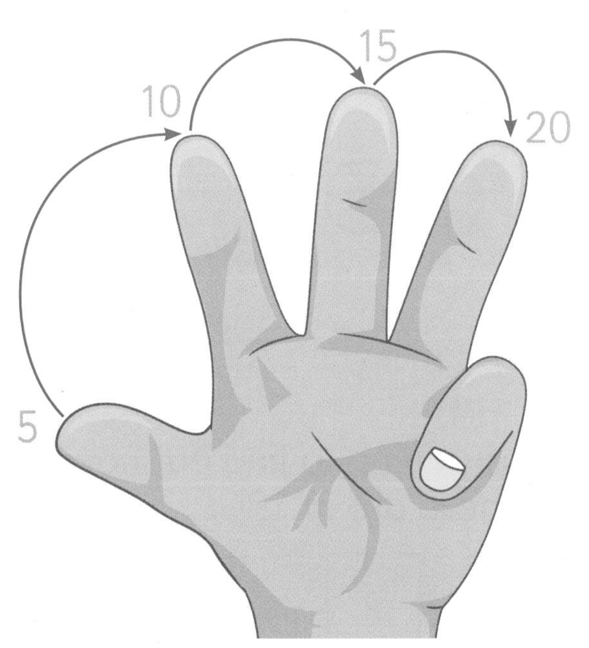

Lesson 7: **Multiplication and division facts for 2, 5 and 10 (1)**

- Find division facts for 2, 5 and 10 from the 2, 5 and 10 times tables

Key words
- division
- multiplication
- times tables

Discover

How could you use the numbers in the triangle to find division facts?

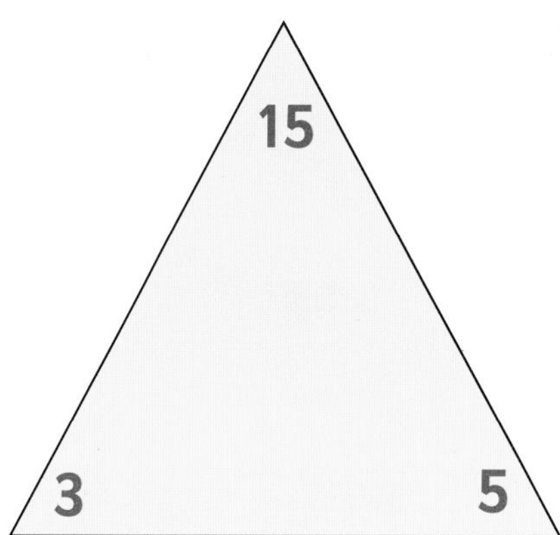

Learn

You can use the numbers in a multiplication number statement to make another multiplication and two divisions to match.

For 8 × 5 = 40

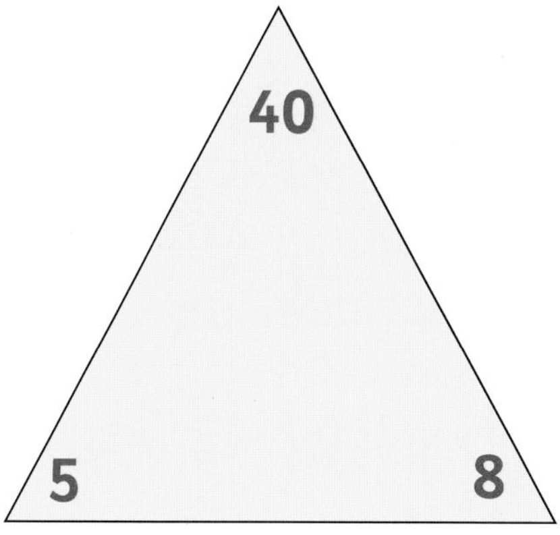

you can write

5 × 8 = 40　　**40 ÷ 5 = 8**　　**40 ÷ 8 = 5**

Lesson 8: **Remainders (1)**

- Share objects into groups to discover if any are left over

Key words
- **divide**
- **share**
- **remainder**

Discover

Not every number can be divided exactly.

Learn

Group a set of objects to find out how many 2s there are in 7.

To work out **7 ÷ 2**, count in 2s to 7 until you cannot make any more groups of 2.

If there are any left over, it is a **remainder**.

Example

How many 2s are there in 9?

9 ÷ 2

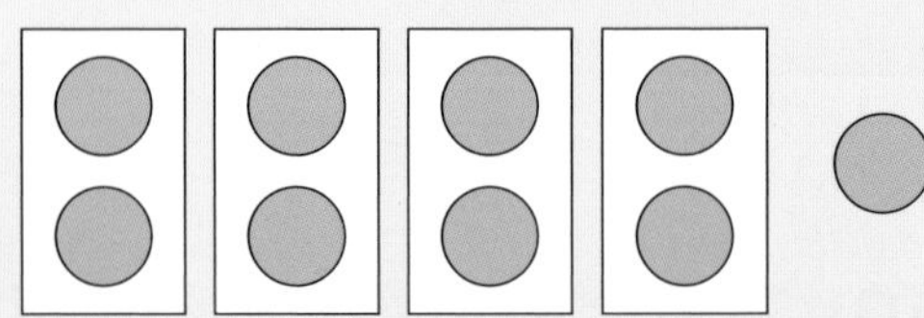

There are 4 groups of 2 with 1 remainder.

Lesson 1: Doubling and halving

- Find doubles and halves

Key words
- multiply
- times
- double
- half

Discover

Learn

To double 25:

Partition:

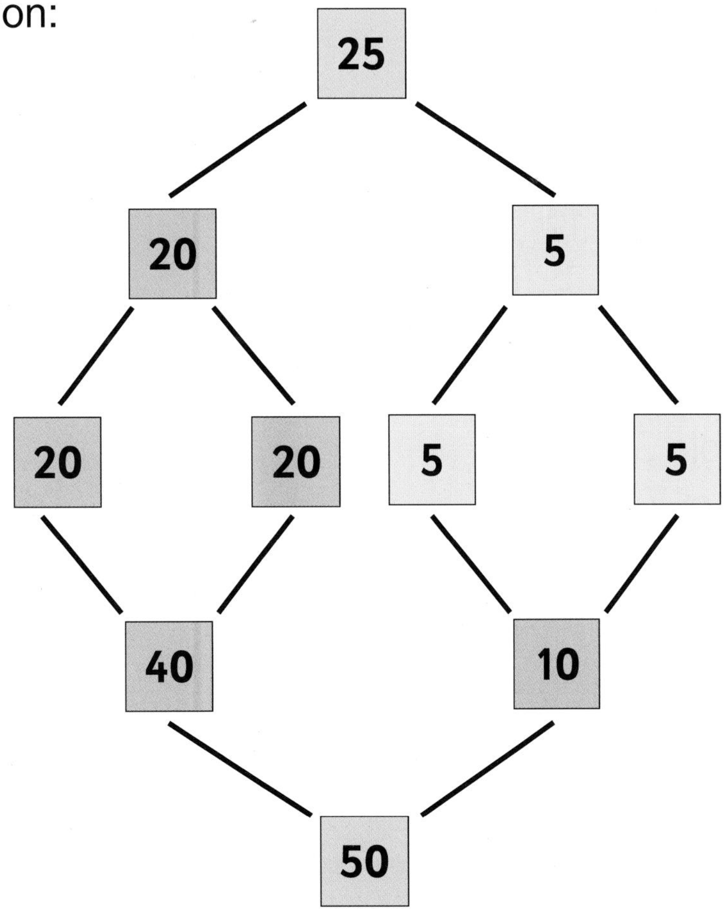

25
20 5
20 20 5 5
40 10
50

Double 20 = 40

Double 5 = 10

40 + 10 = 50

Double 25 = 50
Half of 50 = 25

Lesson 2: Doubles (2)

- Double 2-digit numbers

Key words
- multiply
- times
- double
- partition

Discover

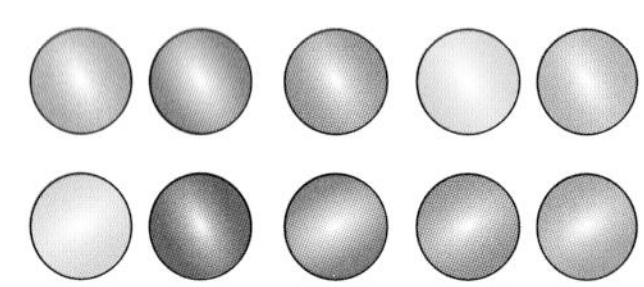

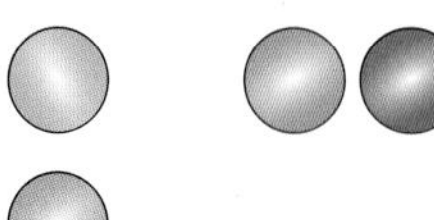

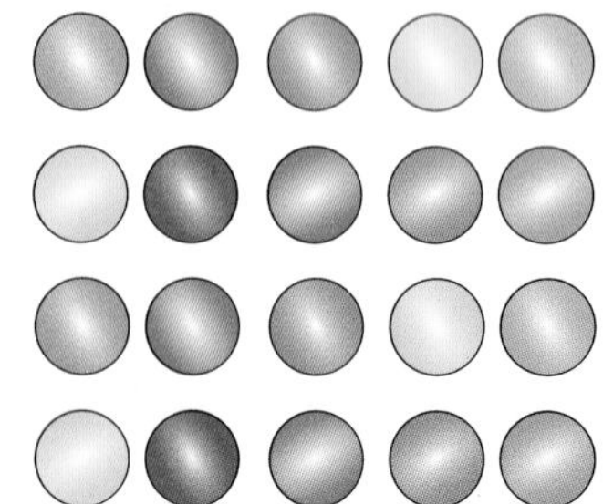

Learn

To double 36: Partition:

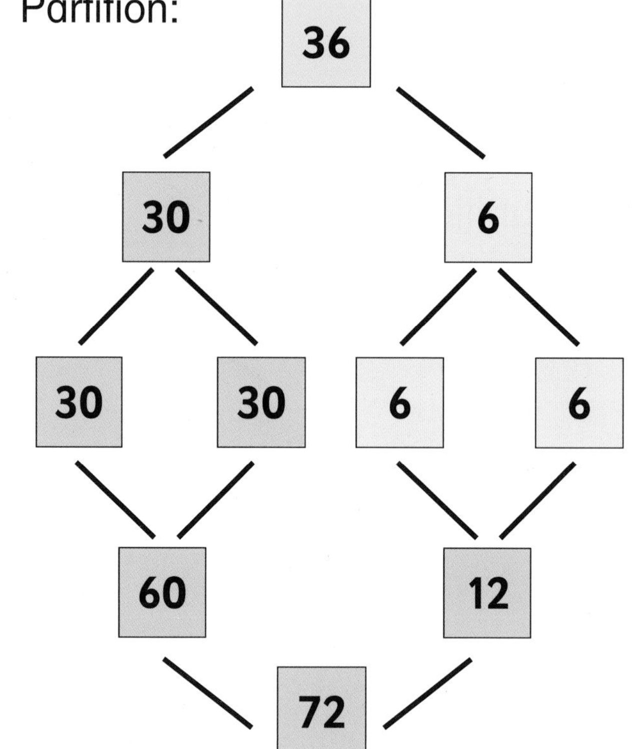

Double 30 = 60
Double 6 = 12

Double 36 = 72
Half of 72 is 36

Example

Use your 100 square to find the double.

Double 23 = 46

Lesson 3: **Multiplication and division facts for 2, 5 and 10 (2)**

- Find division facts for 2, 5 and 10 from the 2, 5 and 10 times tables

Key words
- division
- multiplication
- times tables

Discover

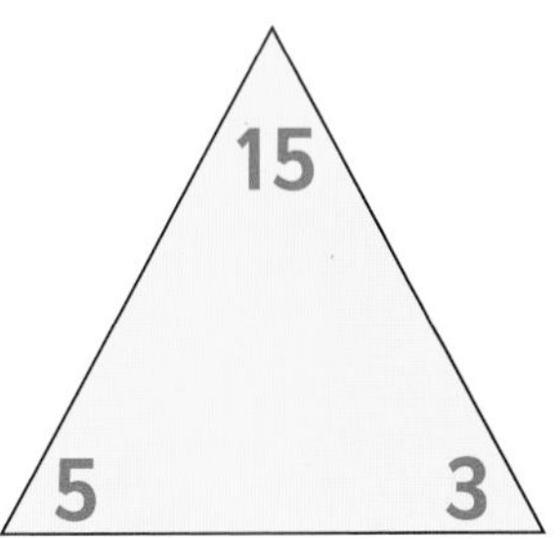

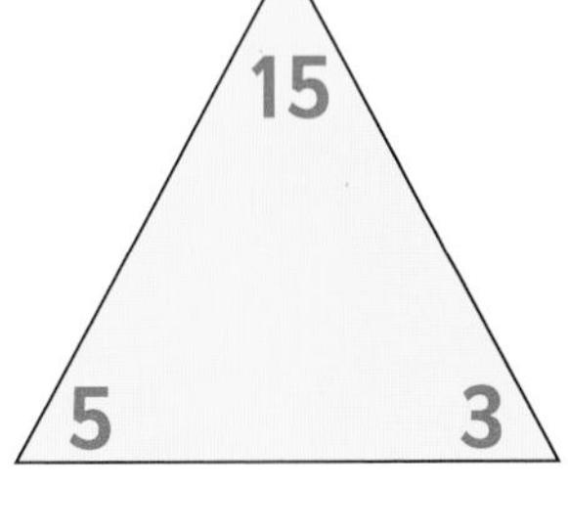

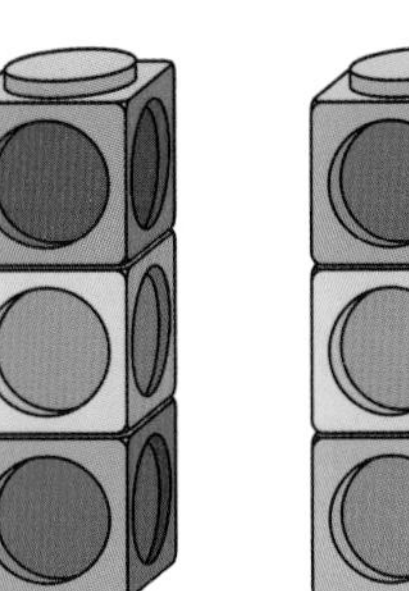

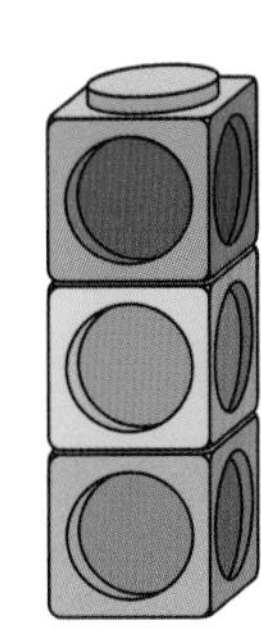

Learn

You can use the numbers in a multiplication number statement to make another multiplication.

$9 \times 2 = 18$ $2 \times 9 = 18$

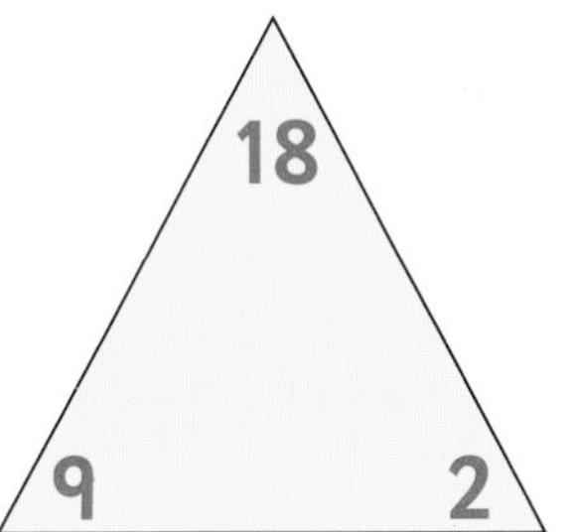

You can also make two division facts.

$18 \div 2 = 9$ $18 \div 9 = 2$

Lesson 4: Multiplication and division facts for the 3× table

- Work out multiplication and division facts for the 3× table

Key words
- division
- multiplication
- times tables

Discover

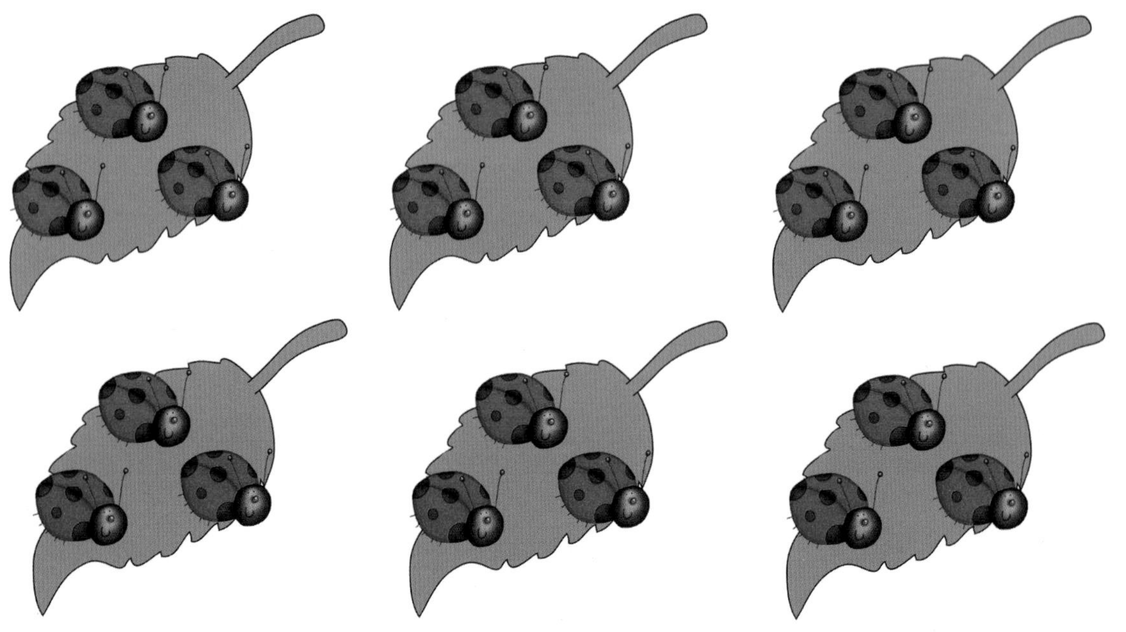

Learn

1	2	3	4	5	6	7	8	9	10
3	6	9	12	15	18	21	24	27	30

Example

Count in 3s on your 100 square to solve this 3s multiplication. Fill in the answer.

5 × 3 = 15

1	2	3	4	5	6	7	8	9	10
11	12	13	14	15	16	17	18	19	20

Lesson 5: **Multiplication and division facts for the 4× table**

- Work out multiplication and division facts for the 4× table

Key words
- division
- multiplication
- times tables

Discover

Learn

1	2	3	4	5	6	7	8	9	10
4	8	12	16	20	24	28	32	36	40

Example

Count in 4s on your 100 square to solve this 4s multiplication. Fill in the answer.

$3 \times 4 =$ 12

1	2	3	4	5	6	7	8	9	10
11	12	13	14	15	16	17	18	19	20

Lesson 6: Remainders (2)

- Solve a division and say how many are left over

Key words
- divide
- division
- share
- remainder

Discover

23 ÷ 5 = ?

Learn

17 ÷ 5 = ?

17 is not a multiple of 5, so there will be some left over when it's shared into 5 groups.

17 ÷ 5 = 3 r2

Lesson 7: **Multiplication and division problems (1)**

- Solve multiplication and division problems

Key words
- division
- multiplication
- times tables

Discover

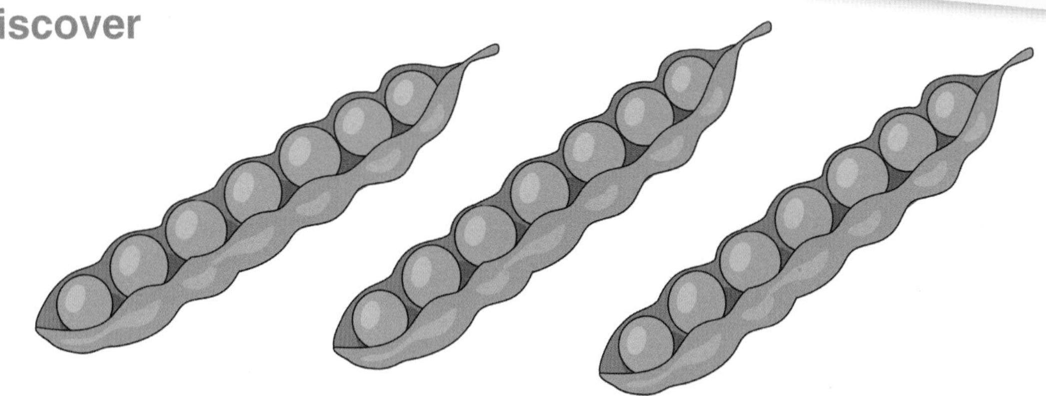

Learn

Multiplication number stories ask you to count groups of objects.

Bananas come in bunches of 5. Sami bought 4 bunches. How many bananas did Sami buy?

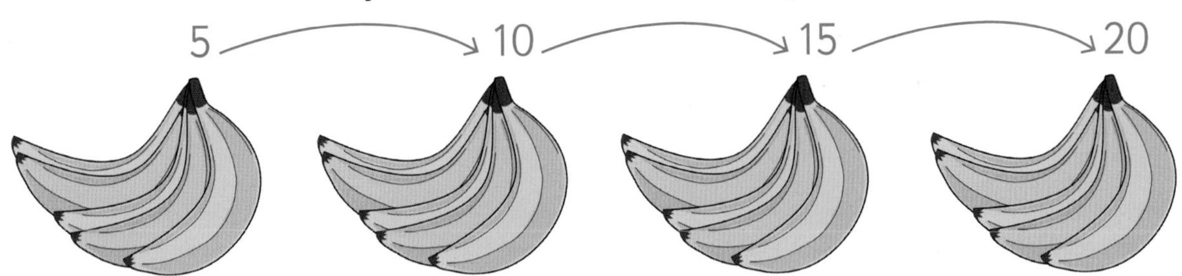

Sami bought 20 bananas. He shared them between 4 friends. How many bananas did each friend get?

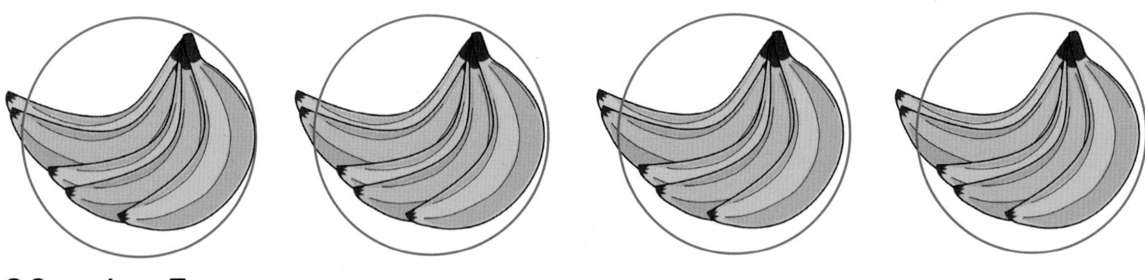

20 ÷ 4 = 5

Lesson 8: **Multiplication and division problems (2)**

- Solve multiplication and division problems

Key words
- groups
- share
- double
- half

Discover

8 ÷ 2 =

Learn

Double means multiply by 2.

Halve means divide by 2.

Example

Solve this problem. Use your 100 square to help you.

I have $4 in my purse. This morning, I had double that amount. How much money did I have this morning?

$8

Lesson 1: **Recognising and naming 2D shapes**

- Recognise and name circles, triangles, squares, rectangles, pentagons and hexagons

Key words
- 2D
- hexagon
- pentagon
- regular
- irregular

Discover

Where have you seen shapes like these in the world around you?

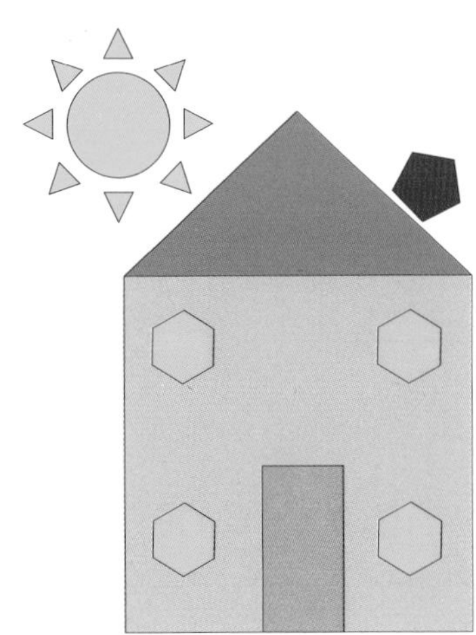

Learn

Circles, rectangles and squares are common 2D shapes, but hexagons and pentagons are also everywhere in the world around us. They can be regular or irregular.

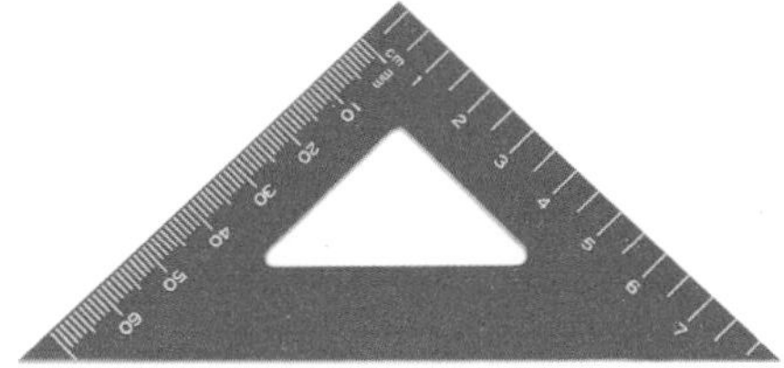

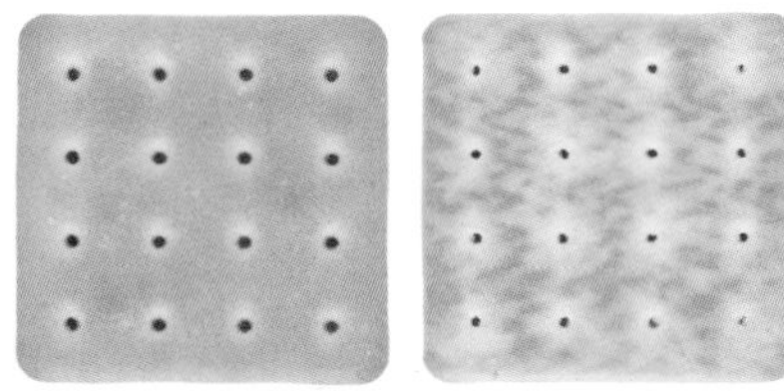

Lesson 2: **Describing 2D shapes**

- Describe 2D shapes by talking about the sides and corners

Key words
- corner
- side
- curved
- straight
- longer
- shorter

Discover

4 corners

4 sides

Learn

A shape's properties help you describe it.

Shape	Regular	Irregular	Sides	Corners
circle			1 side	no corners
rectangle			4 sides	4 corners
square			4 sides the same length	4 corners
pentagon			5 sides	5 corners
hexagon			6 sides	6 corners

Lesson 3: **Visualising and drawing 2D shapes**

- Imagine a 2D shape and draw it

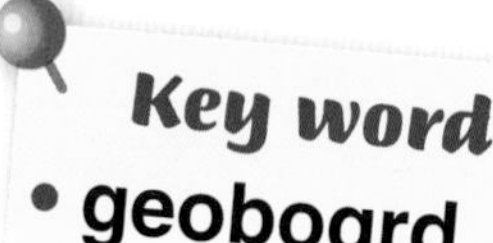

Discover

Learn

Use a geoboard or squared paper, pencil and a ruler to draw 2D shapes.

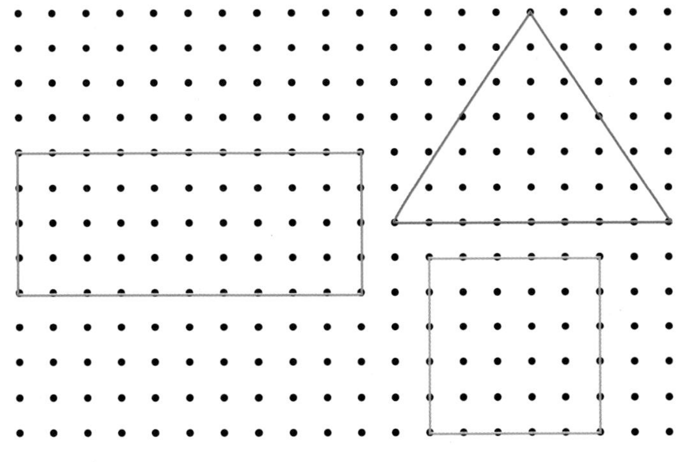

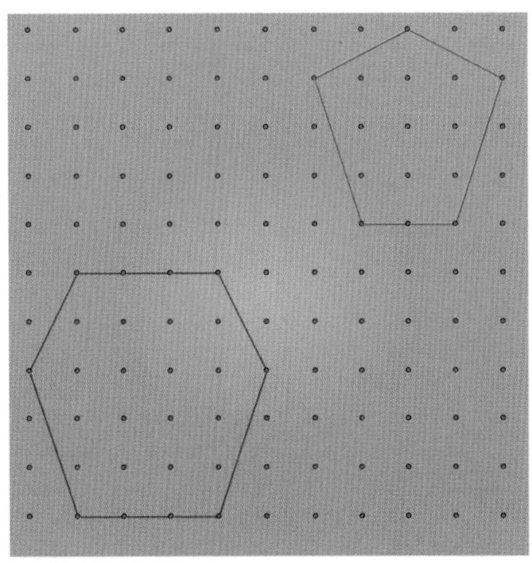

Lesson 4: **Sorting 2D shapes**

- Compare and sort 2D shapes

Key words
- compare
- sorting rule
- side
- corner
- regular
- irregular

Discover

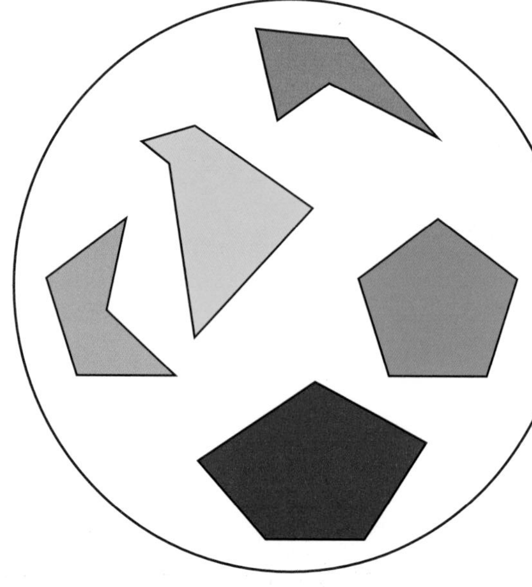

Pentagons – 5 sides

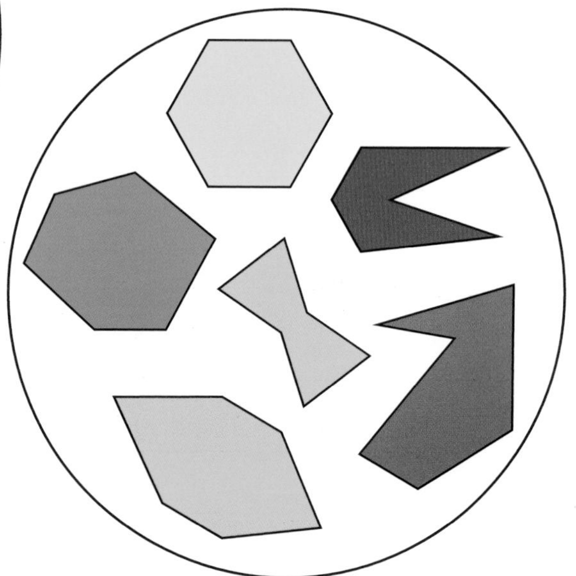

Hexagons – 6 sides

Learn

To sort 2D shapes, use a sorting rule. The results will depend on the sorting rule.

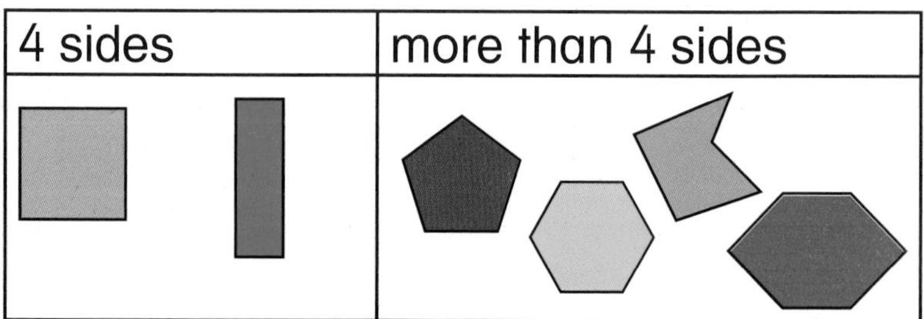

4 sides	more than 4 sides

sides the same	sides not the same

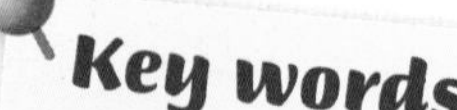

Lesson 1: **Recognising and naming 3D shapes**

- Recognise and name spheres, cones, cylinders, cubes, cuboids and pyramids

Key words
- sphere
- cone
- cylinder
- cube
- cuboid
- pyramid

Discover

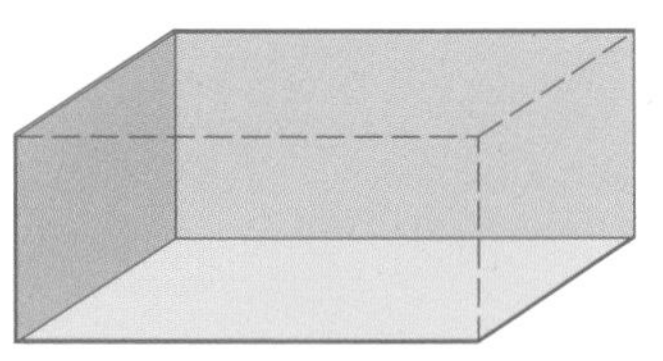

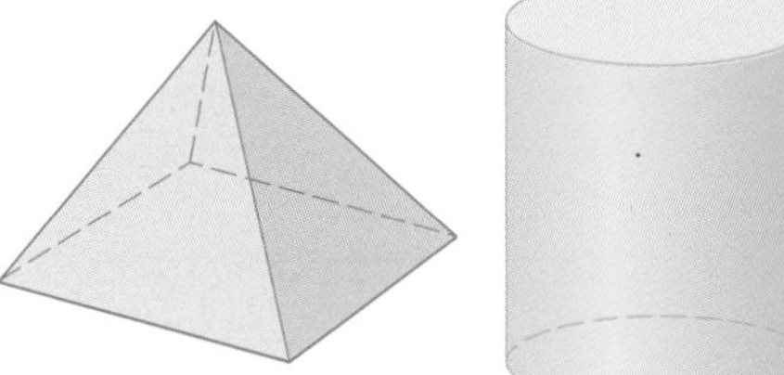

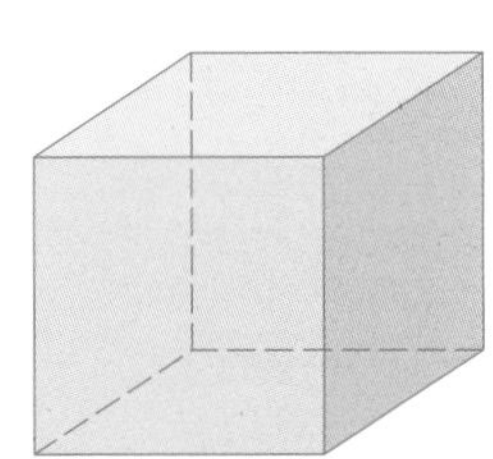

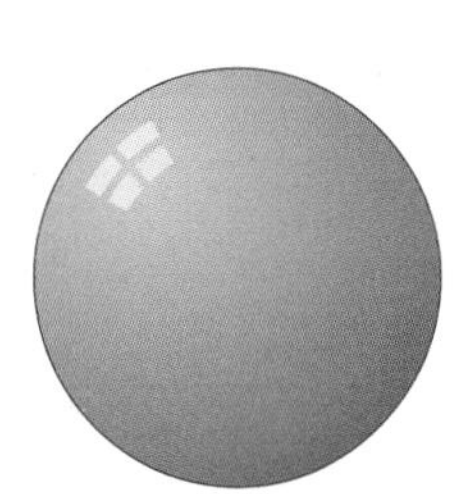

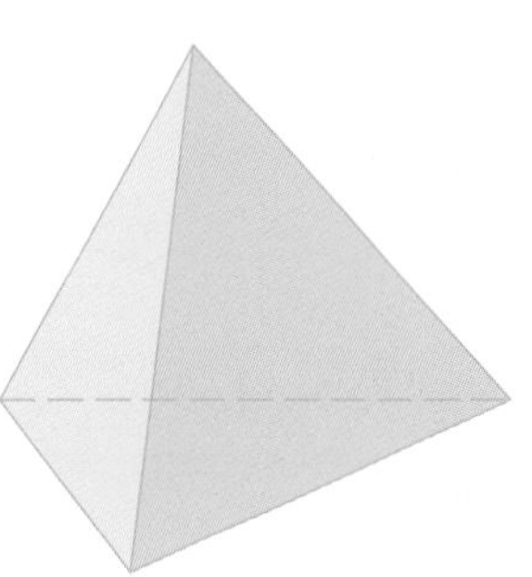

Learn

3D shapes have height, length and width. They are in the world around us.

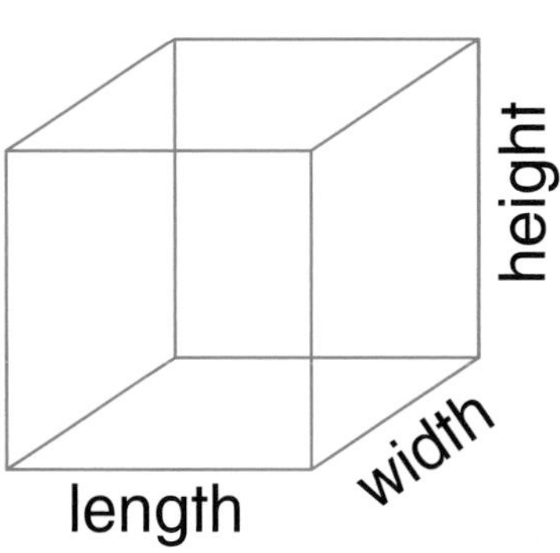

3D shape	Real life
sphere	
cuboid	
cylinder	
cone	
pyramid	

Lesson 2: **Describing 3D shapes**

- Talk about the faces, corners and edges of 3D shapes

Key words
- face
- corner
- edge

Discover

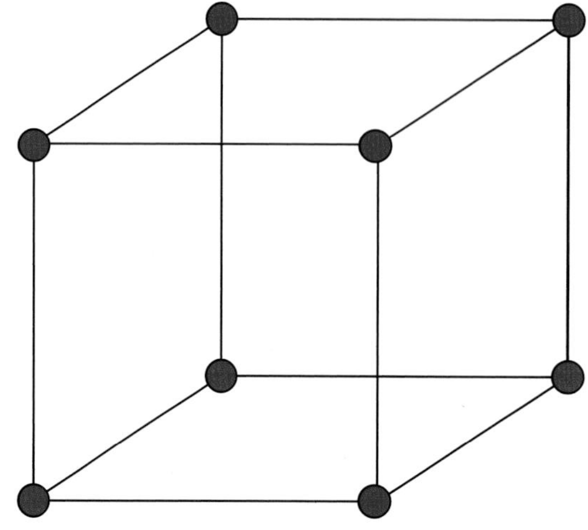

Learn

Every 3D shape can be described by its faces, edges and corners.

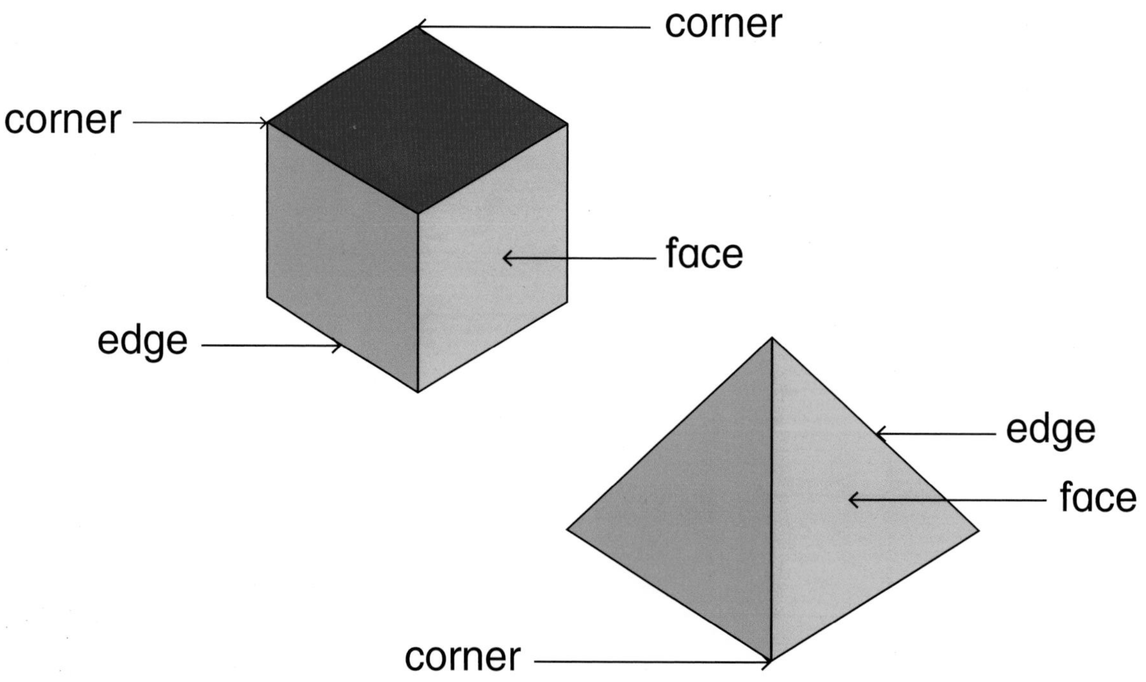

Lesson 3: **Making 3D shapes**

- Make 3D shapes

Key words

- face
- corner
- edge
- model
- base

Discover

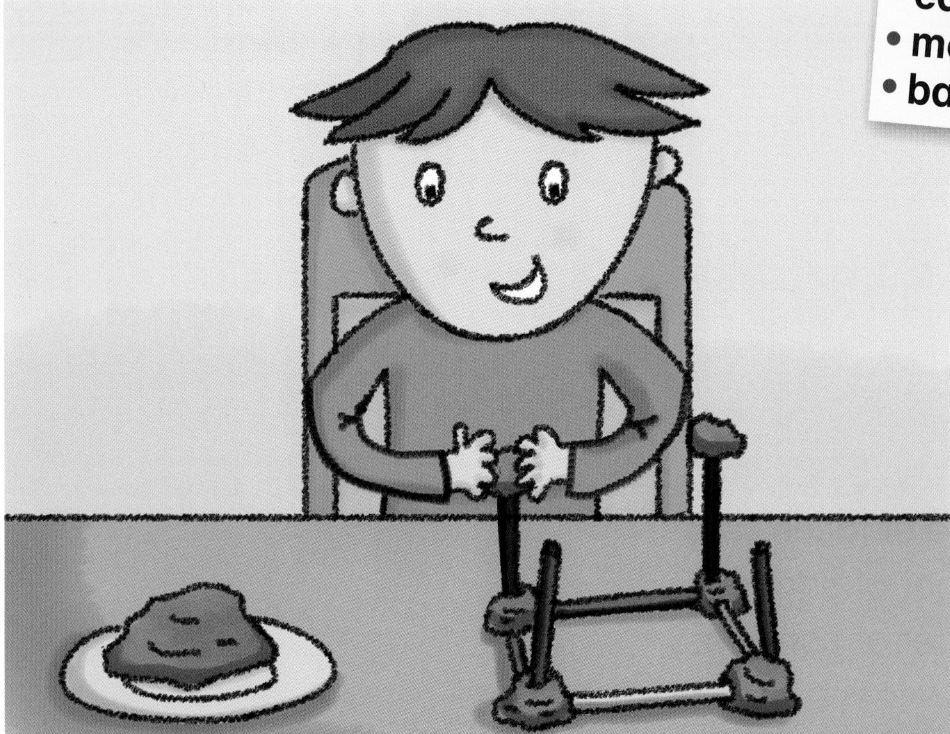

Learn

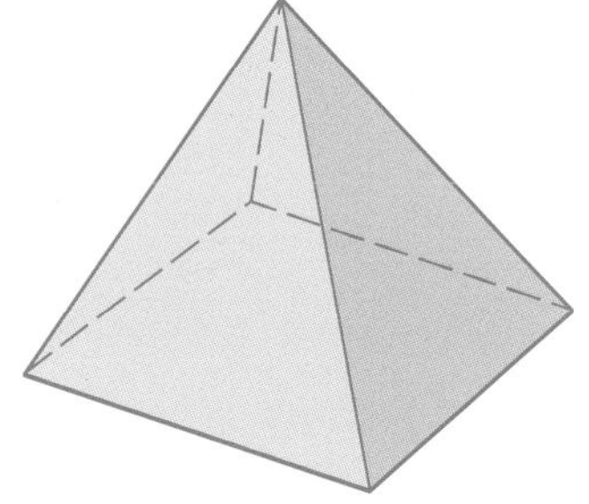

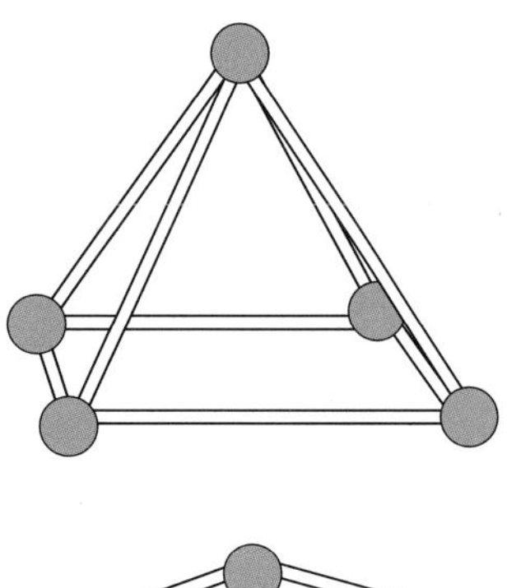

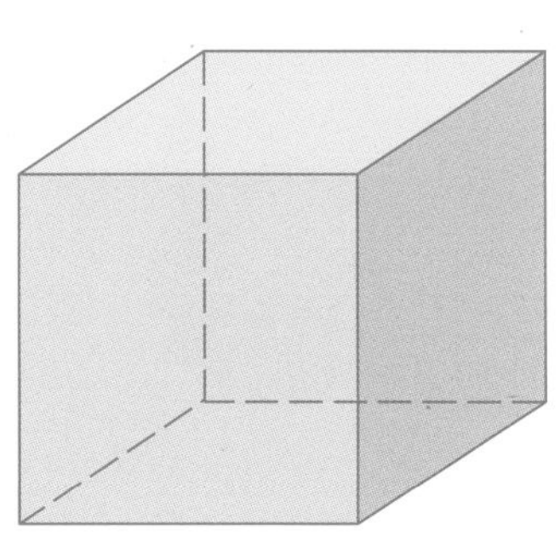

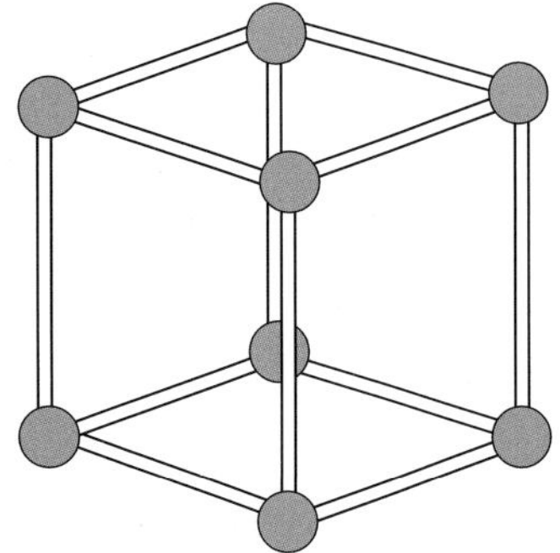

Lesson 4: **Sorting 3D shapes**

- Compare and sort 3D shapes

Key words

- face
- edge
- corner
- flat
- curved
- same
- different

Discover

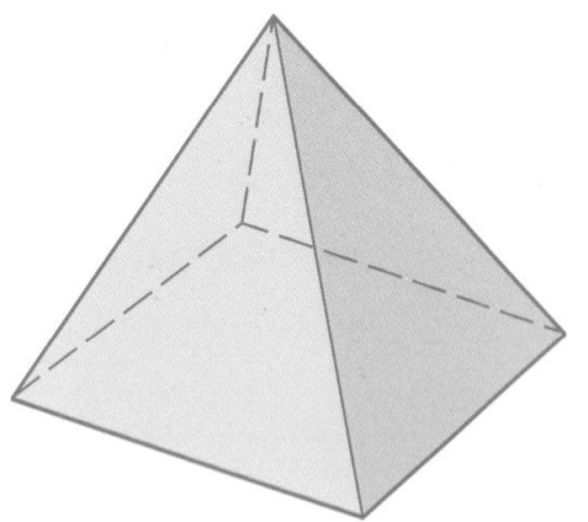

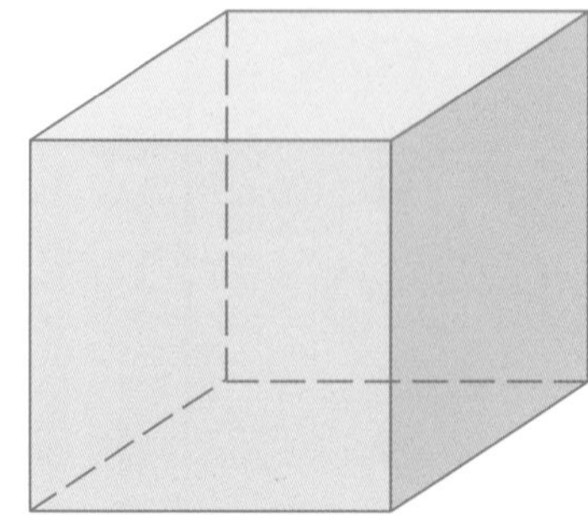

Learn

Compare shapes by looking at:

- the shape of faces
- the number of edges
- the number of corners.

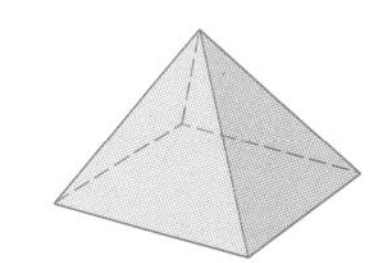

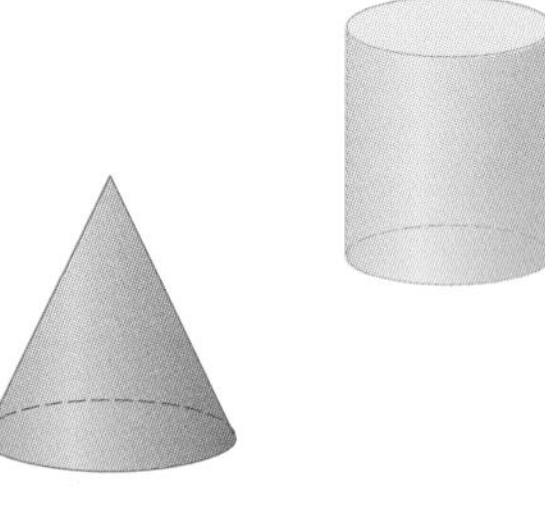

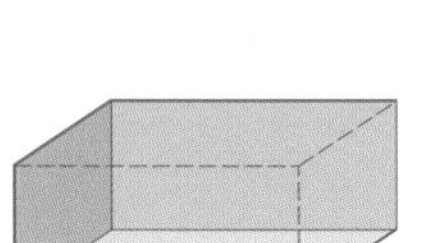

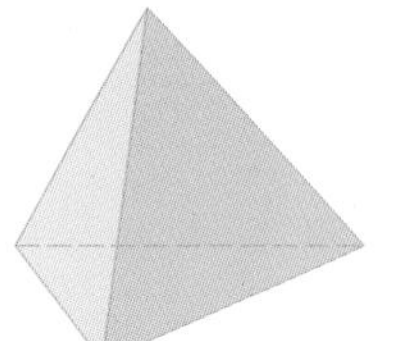

Sort by face shape.

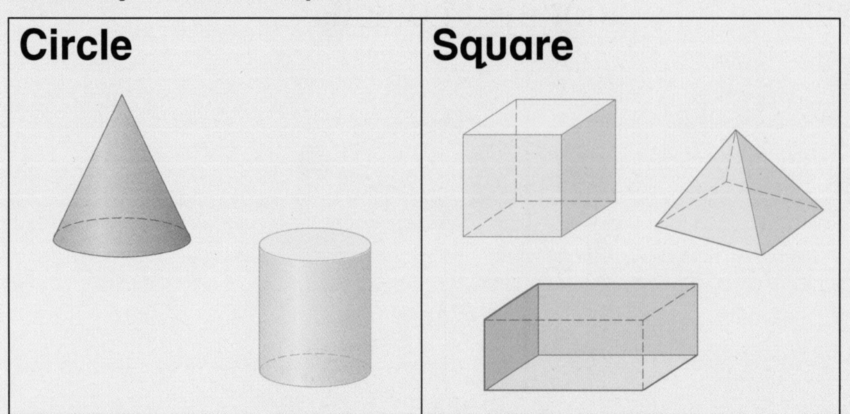

Lesson 1: **Symmetry in patterns**

- Recognise symmetry in patterns

Key words
- line of symmetry
- mirror image
- same
- pattern

Discover

Learn

symmetrical

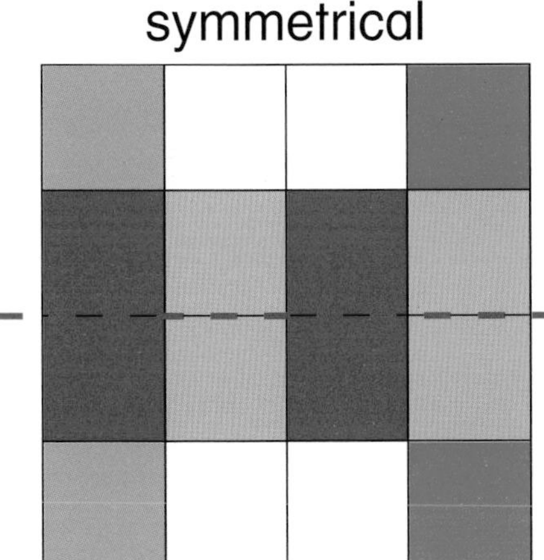

symmetrical

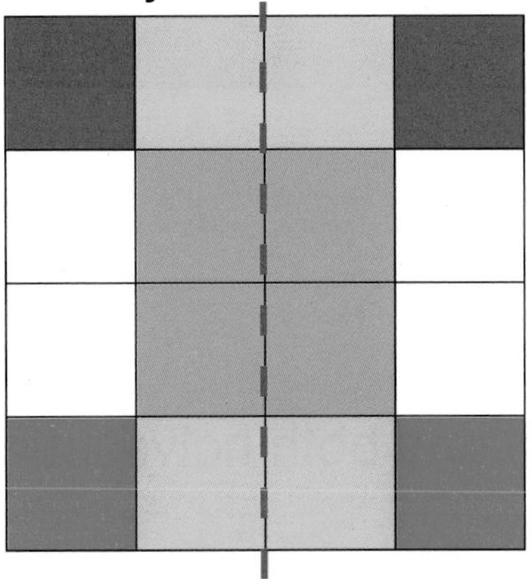

not symmetrical

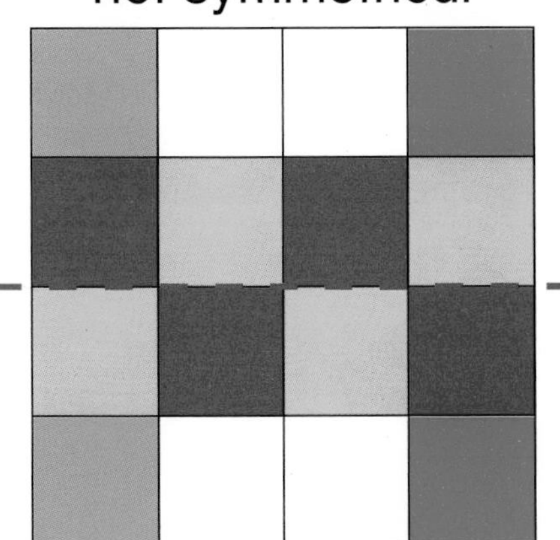

not symmetrical

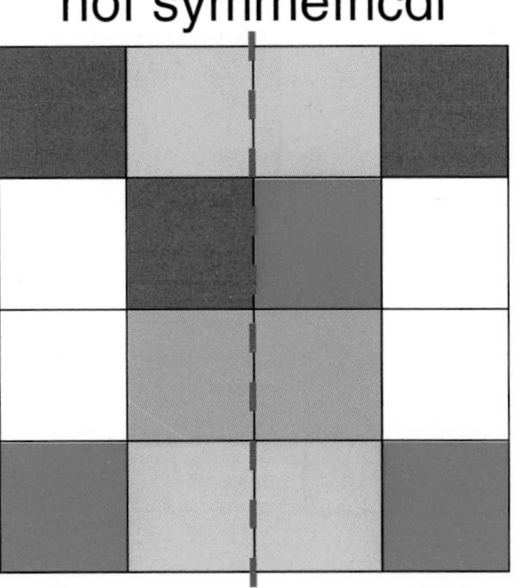

Lesson 2: **Symmetry in 2D shapes**

• Recognise symmetry in 2D shapes

Key words
- line of symmetry
- mirror image
- vertical
- horizontal
- diagonal

Discover

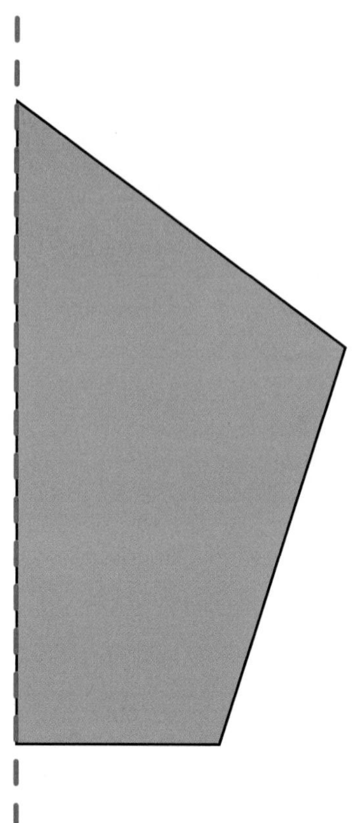

Learn

These shapes have reflective symmetry. You can fold them along the centre and both halves match.

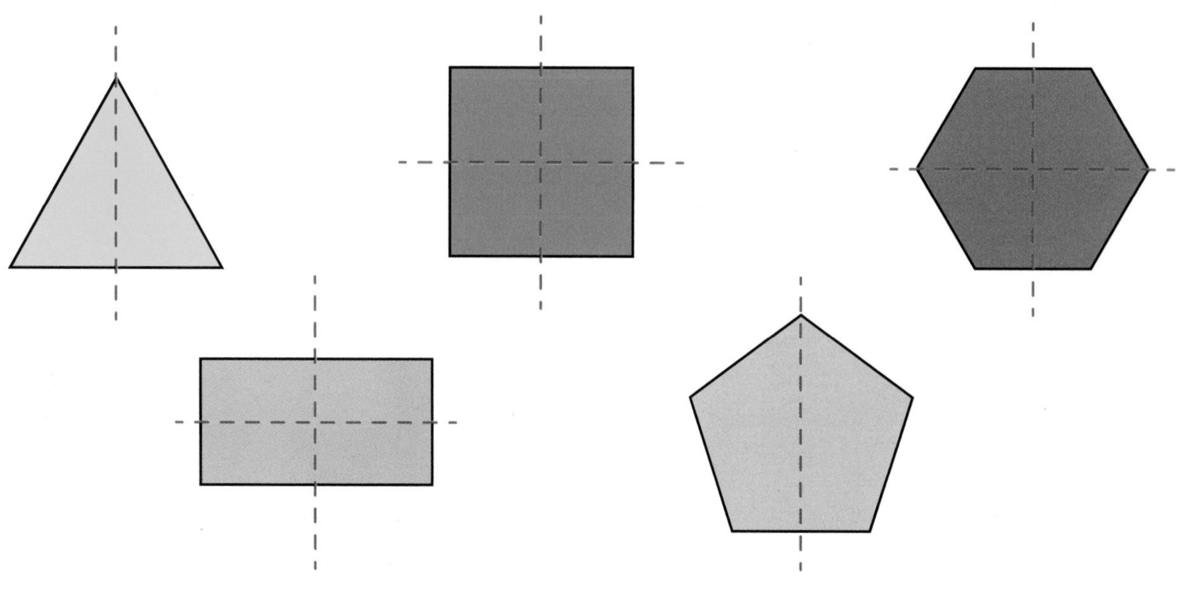

- Draw horizontal and vertical lines of symmetry

Key words
- line of symmetry
- straight
- horizontal
- vertical

Discover

How many lines of symmetry can you see?

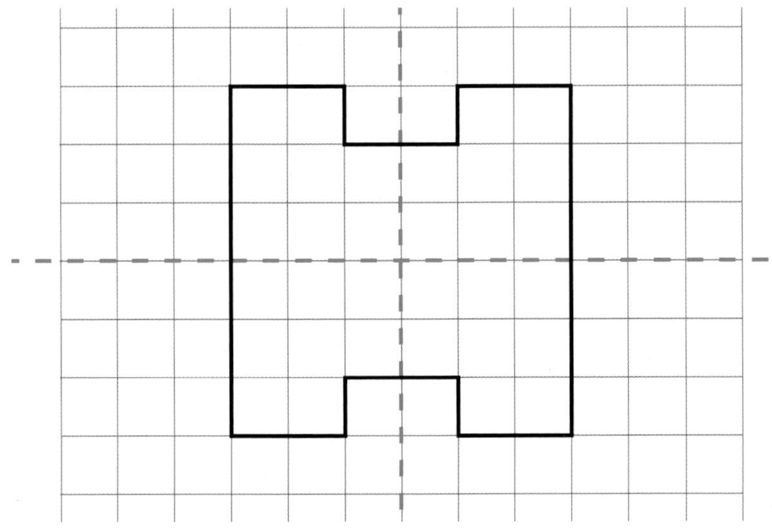

Learn

You can draw a horizontal, vertical or diagonal line of symmetry.

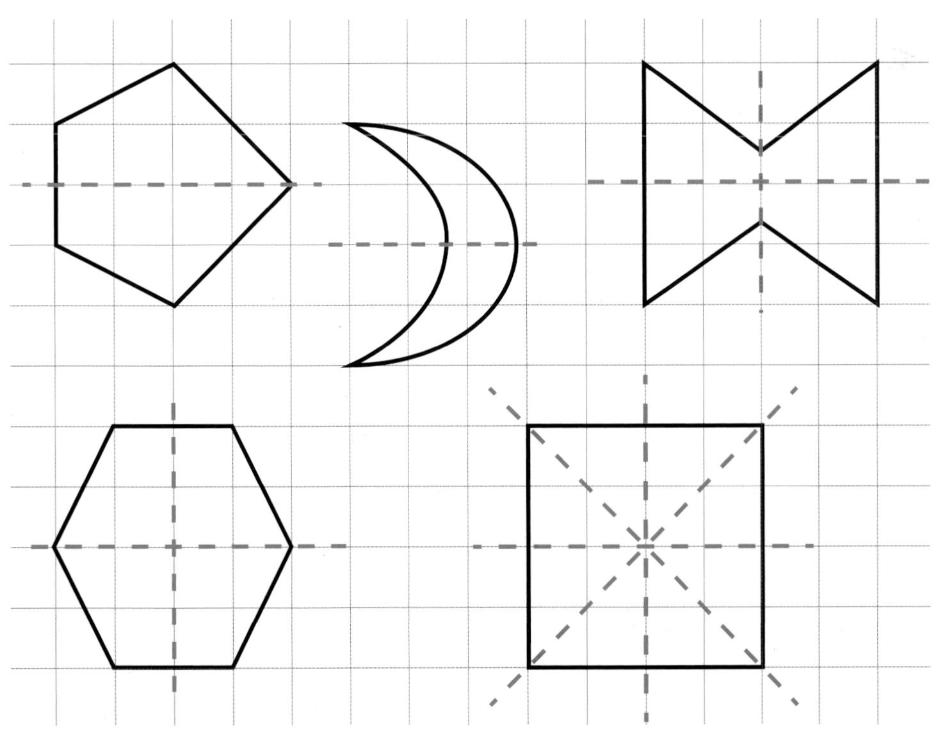

Geometry

Lesson 4: **Symmetry all around us**

- Recognise when an everyday object has one or more lines of symmetry

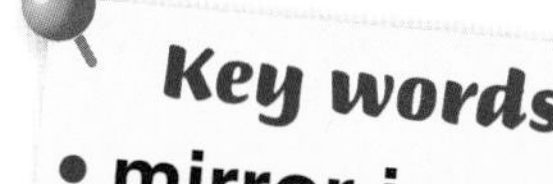

Key words
- **mirror image**
- **line of symmetry**

Discover

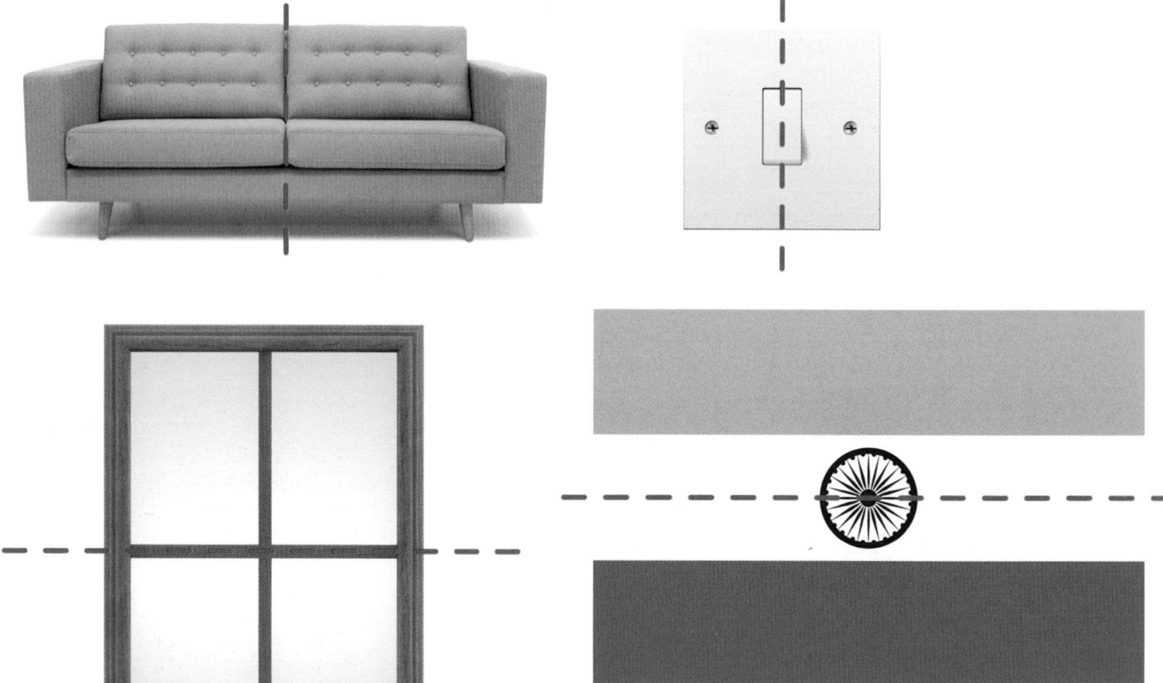

Learn

Lines of symmetry are all around us.

Lesson 1: **Position**

- Follow and give instructions for position

Key words
- in front of
- next to
- top
- middle
- below
- underneath
- corner

Discover

The [goat] is behind the [tree].

top

underneath

in the middle

below

behind

in front of

next to

on

Learn

Meet me on the corner, in front of the café. I'll be standing next to the traffic lights.

Lesson 2: Direction and movement

- Follow and give directions to move from one position to another

Key words
- left
- right
- through
- straight
- forwards
- go back

Discover

Learn

You can follow directions to move from one place to another.

1	Go forward 1	↑ 1
2	1 step left	← 1
3	Face right	R
4	2 steps forward	↑ 2
5	1 step right	→ 1
6	Face left	L
7	Go forward 1	↑ 1
8	3 steps right	→ 3

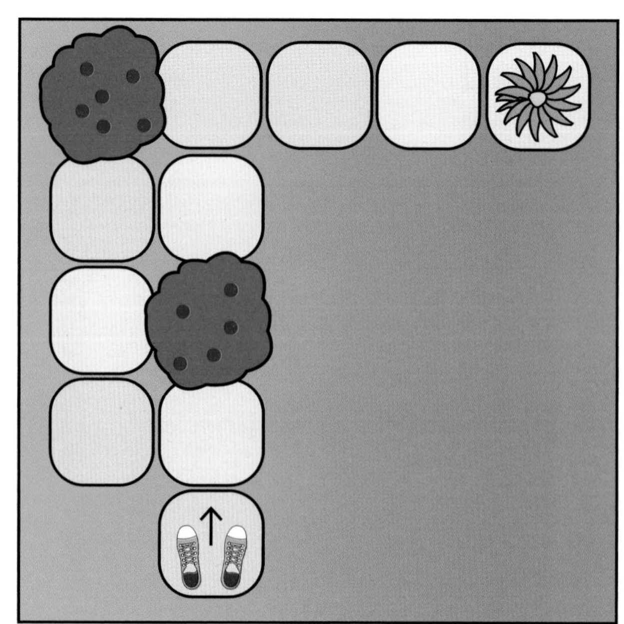

Lesson 3: **Whole, half and quarter turns**

- Make whole, half and quarter turns clockwise and anticlockwise

Key words

- whole turn
- half turn
- quarter turn
- clockwise
- anticlockwise

Discover

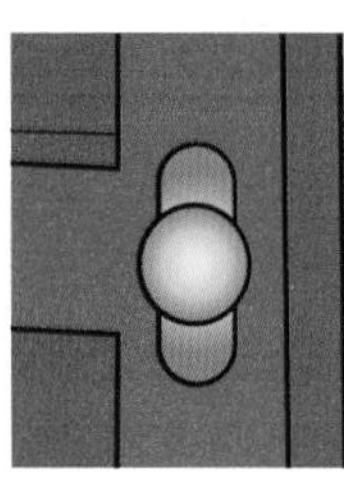

Learn

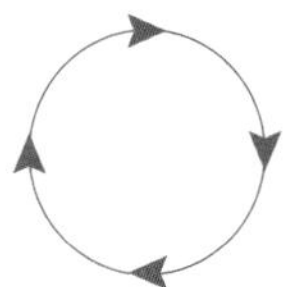
clockwise direction

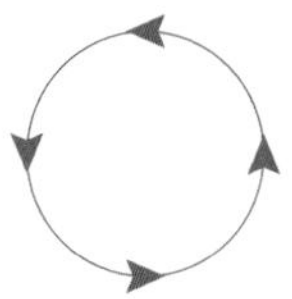
anticlockwise direction

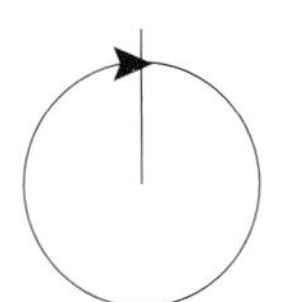
whole turn

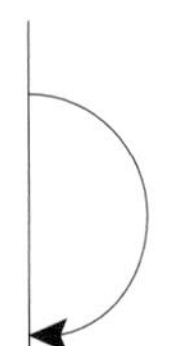
$\frac{1}{2}$ turn

$\frac{1}{4}$ turn

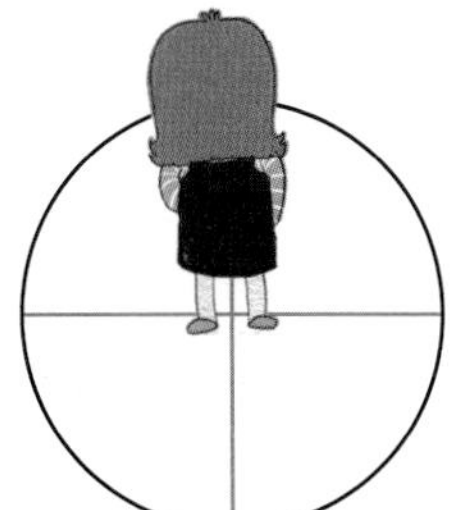

Lesson 4: **Right angles**

- Recognise a quarter turn is a right angle

Key words
- right angle
- quarter turn
- clockwise
- anticlockwise
- left
- right

Discover

Learn

Right angles can be in any position. They are the same as a quarter turn.

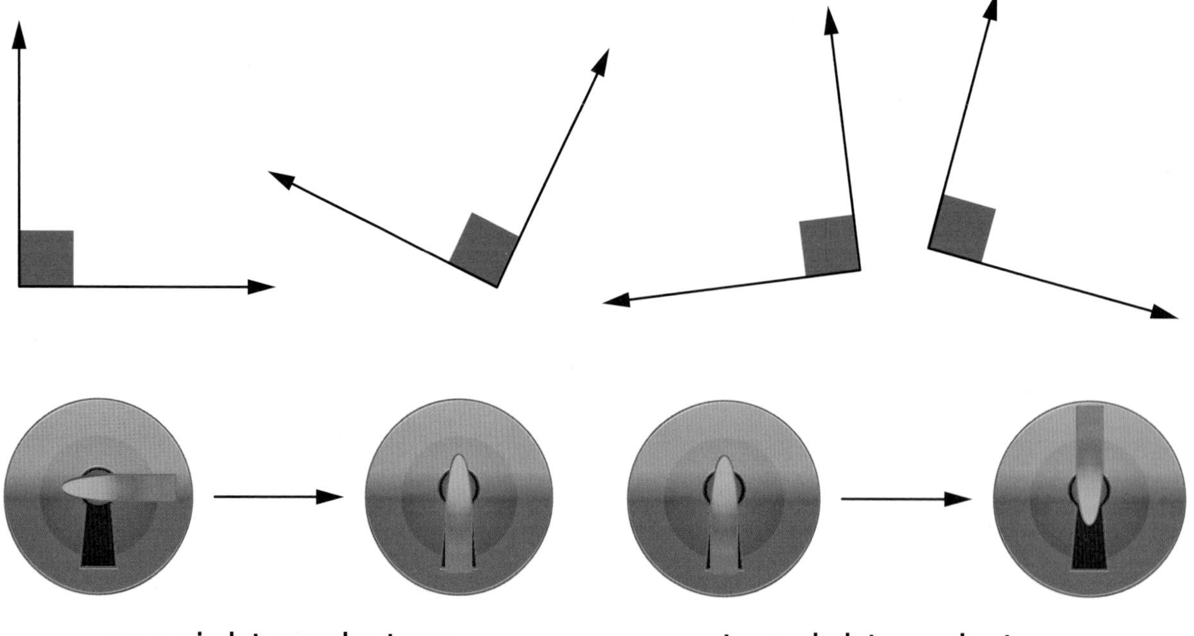

one right angle turn

two right angle turns

Lesson 1: **Recognising all coins and notes**

- Recognise all coins and notes

Key words
- cent
- dollar
- value

Discover

Learn

You can make amounts of money in different ways.

1c
one cent

5c
five cents

10c
ten cents

25c
twenty-five cents

50c
fifty cents

$1
one dollar

$2
two dollars

$5
five dollars

$10
ten dollars

$20
twenty dollars

$50
fifty dollars

$100
hundred dollars

Lesson 2: **Finding totals (1)**

- Find totals of up to 50c and $20

Key words

- total value
- amount
- price

Discover

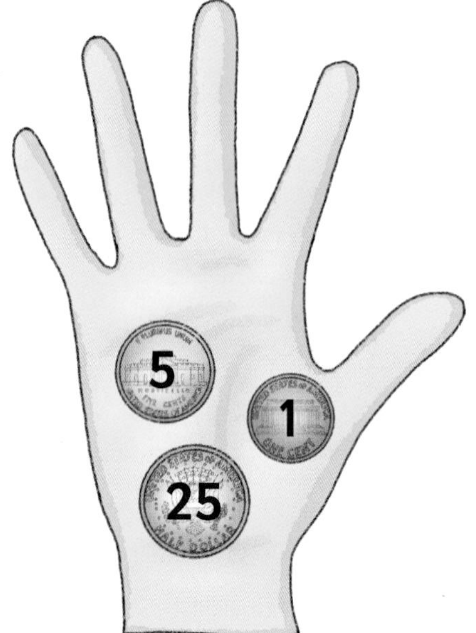

Learn

Lesson 3: **Finding totals to pay an amount (1)**

- Make totals up to 50c and $20 to pay an exact amount

Key words
- change
- total value
- amount
- cost

Discover

Learn

Lesson 4: **Finding totals and working out change (1)**

- Find totals and give change

Key words
- change
- total value
- amount
- cost

Discover

Learn

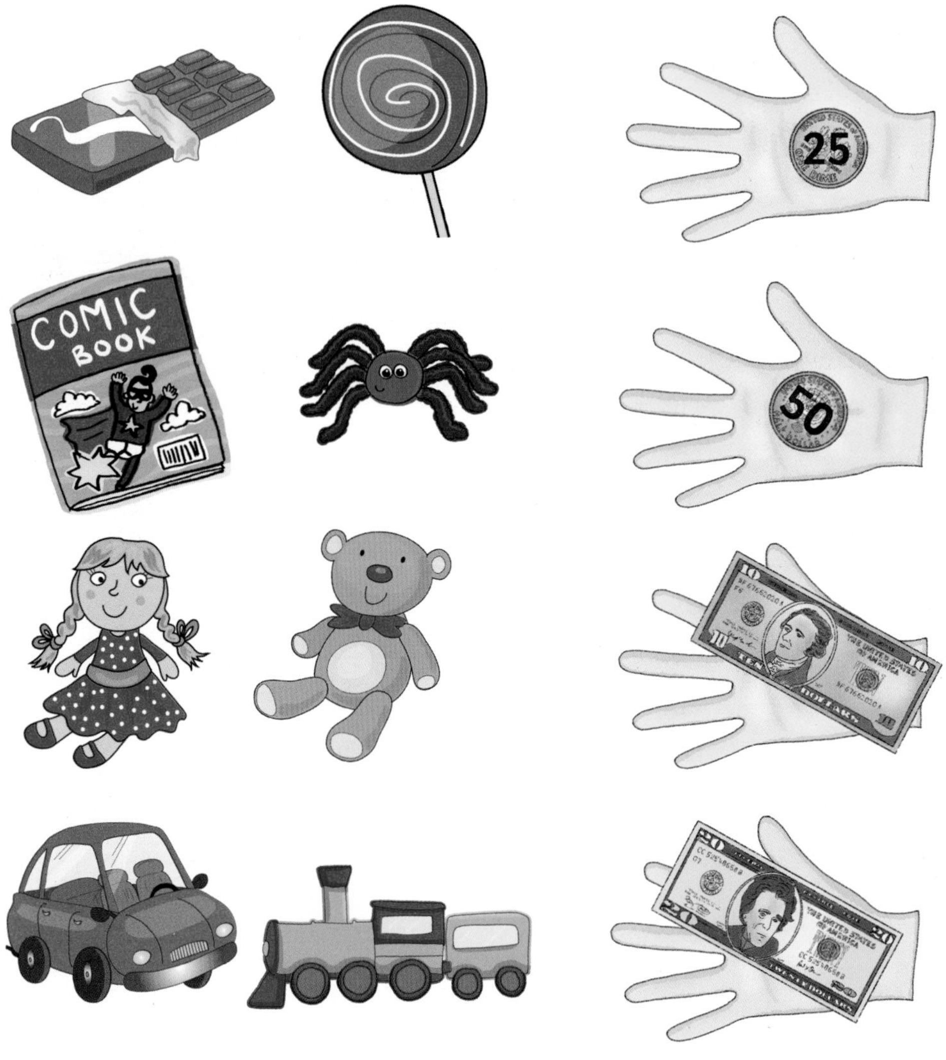

Lesson 1: **Finding totals (2)**

- Recognise all coins and notes and find totals

Key words
- cent
- dollar

Discover

Learn

Lesson 2: **Finding totals to pay an amount (2)**

- Find totals in coins and notes to pay an exact amount

Key words
- total value
- exact amount
- cost
- price

Discover

50c

Learn

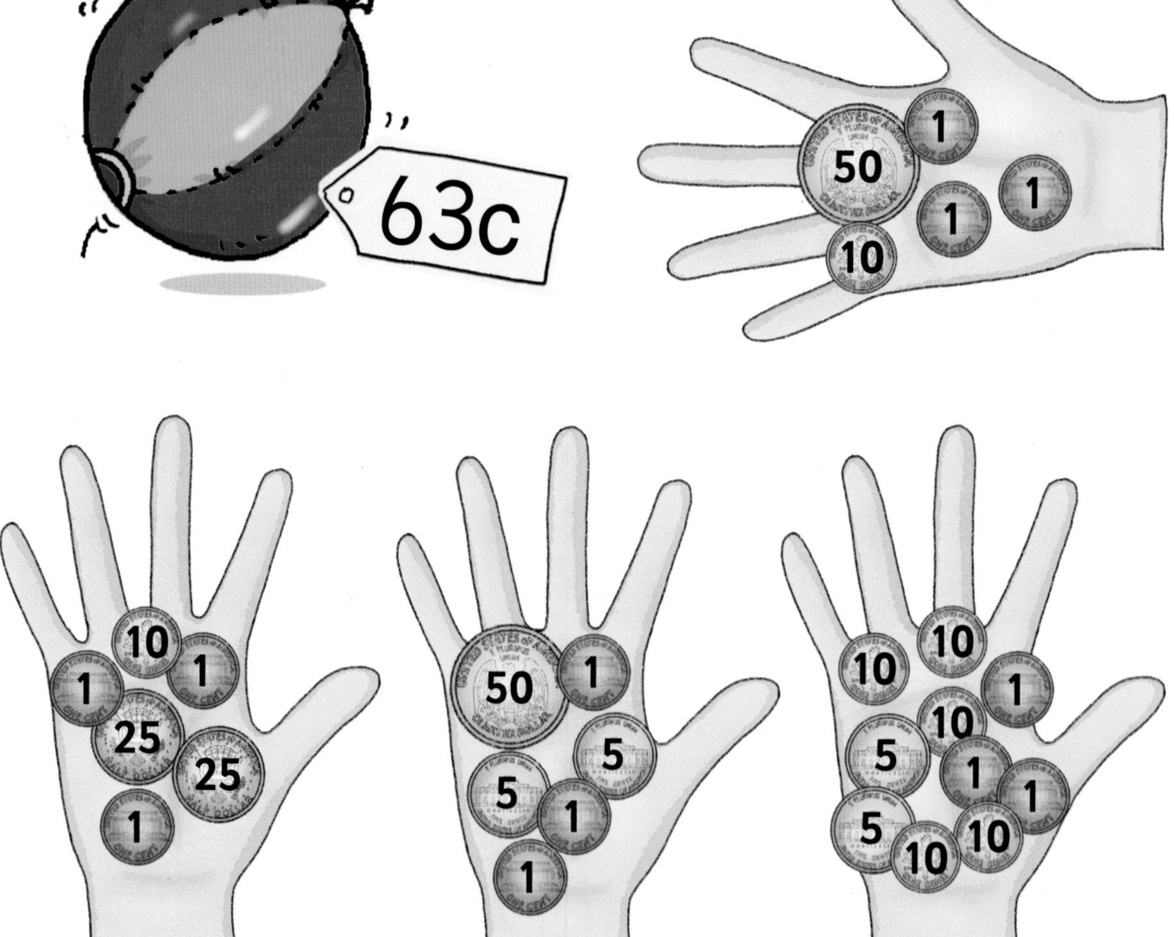

Measure

Lesson 3: **Finding totals and working out change (2)**

- Find totals in coins and notes and work out change

Key words
- total value
- amount
- cost
- price
- change

Discover

Learn

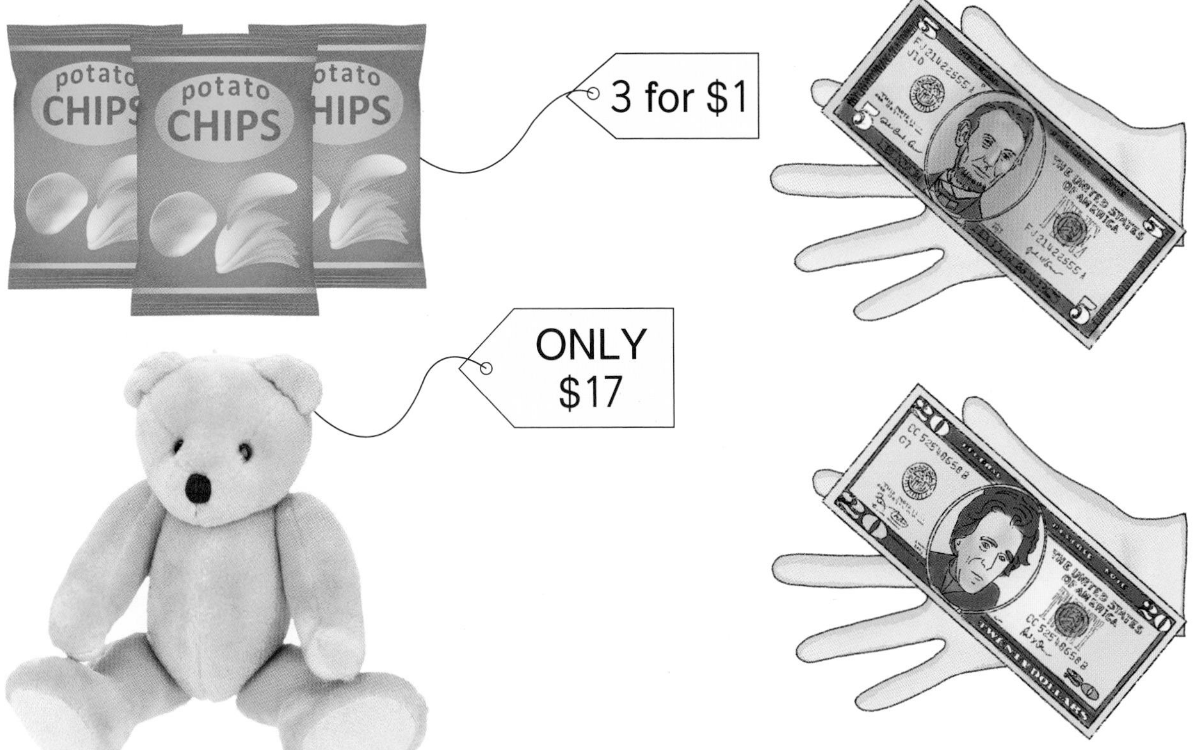

Lesson 4: **Finding totals and working out change (3)**

- Find totals and work out change for money word problems

Key words
- total value
- amount
- cost
- price
- change

Discover

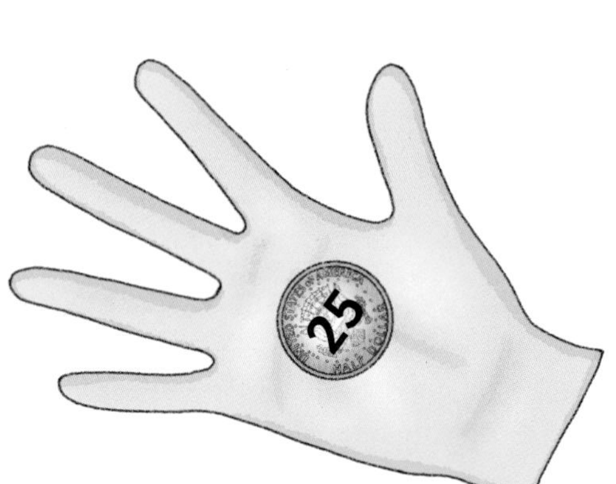

Learn

Lesson 1: **Measuring lengths and choosing non-standard units**

- Estimate and measure length with units of measure that are the same

Key words

- **length**
- **estimate**
- **measure**
- **unit of measure**
- **more than**
- **less than**

Discover

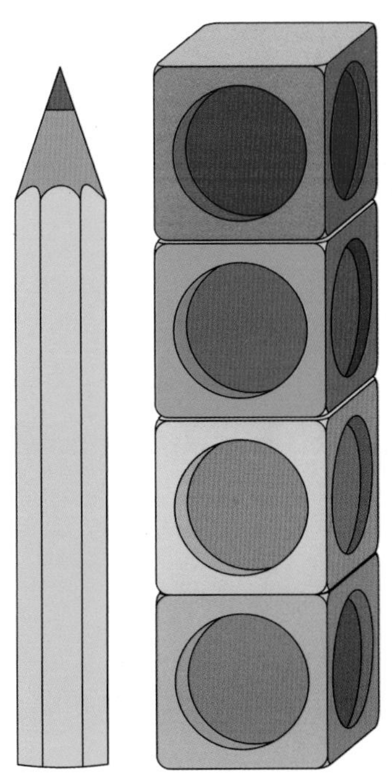

Learn

The ribbon is 31 interlocking cubes, or 6 lolly sticks in length.

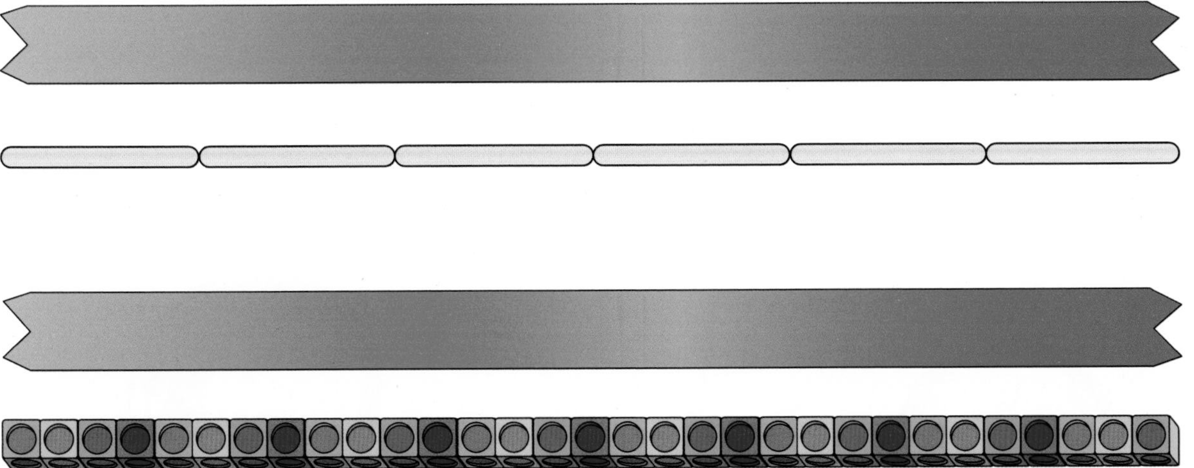

Measure

Lesson 2: **Standard units: metre, centimetre**

- Recognise and use the standard units: metre and centimetre

Key words
- metre
- centimetre
- ruler
- metre rule

Discover

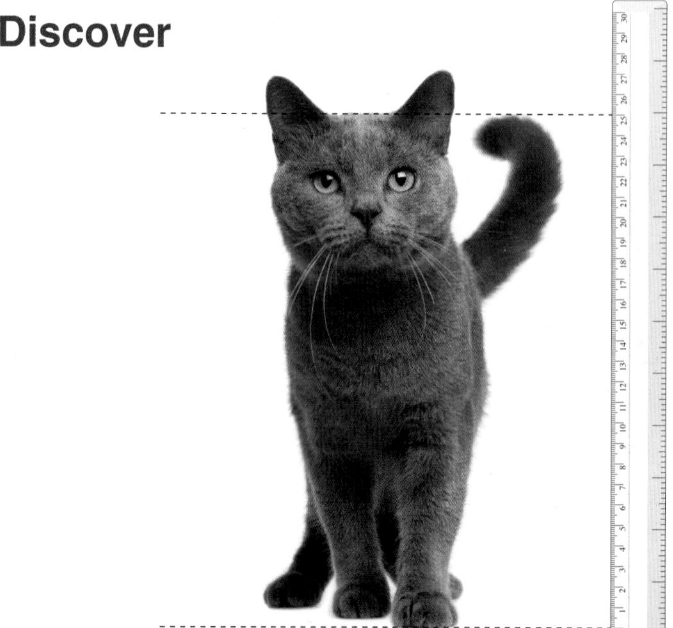

Learn

1 metre = 100 centimetres.

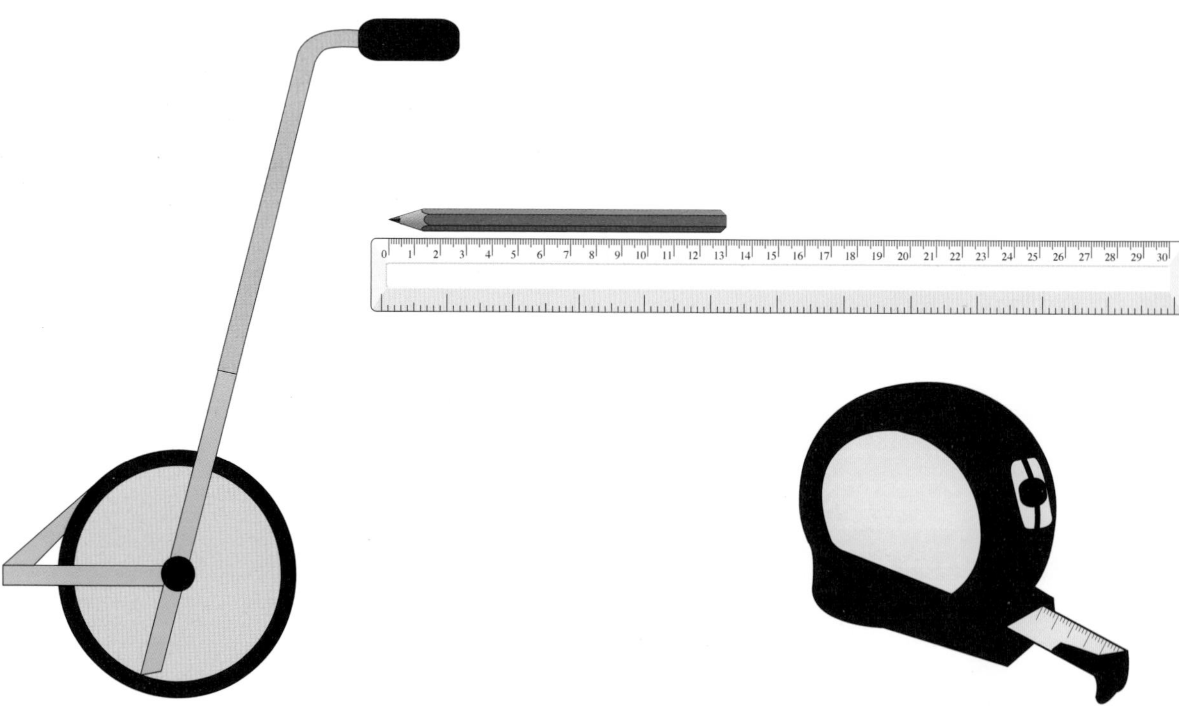

Lesson 3: **Choosing suitable standard units: length**

- Estimate and measure length in centimetres and metres, choosing the best unit and instrument

Key word

- **measuring instrument**

Discover

Learn

Measuring tools.

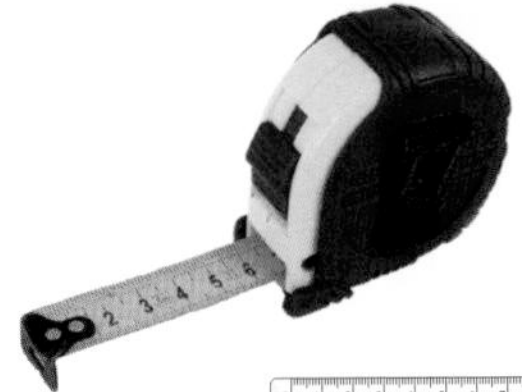

How would you measure these?

Measure

Lesson 4: **Comparing lengths**

• Use a ruler to compare lengths

Key words
- compare
- shortest
- longest

Discover

Learn

Compare these lengths to find the shortest and longest.

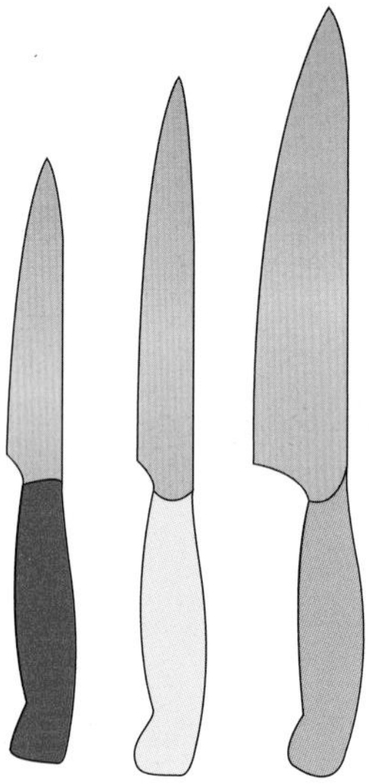

Lesson 1: **Measuring weights and choosing non-standard units**

- Estimate and measure weights with units of measure that are the same

Key words
- weight
- unit of measure
- level
- balanced

Discover

Learn

To weigh an object, add units of measure until the scales balance. Then count the units.

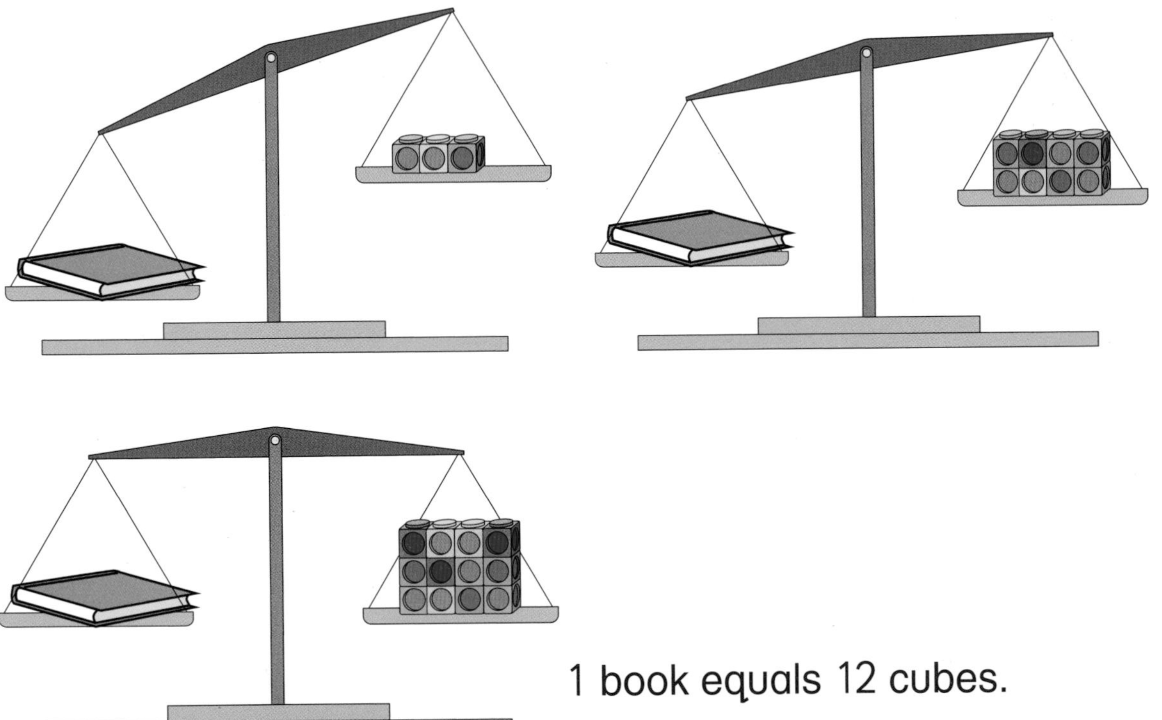

1 book equals 12 cubes.

Lesson 2: **Standard units: kilogram and gram**

- Recognise and use the standard units: kilogram and gram

Key words

- **gram (g)**
- **100 g**
- **kilogram (kg)**
- **1 kg**

Discover

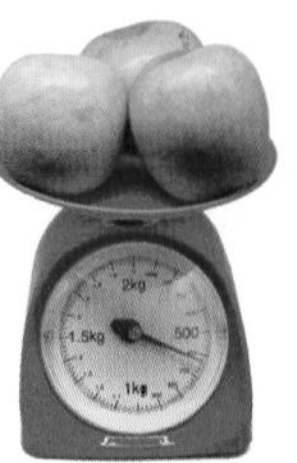

Learn

These weigh about 1 g.

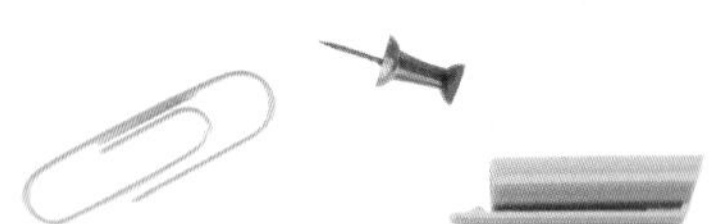

These weigh about 1 kg.

These are measured in hundreds of grams.

1000 g = 1 kg

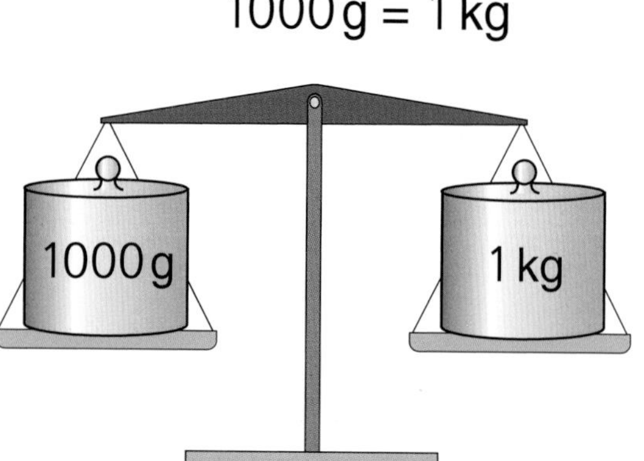

1 kg = 10 × 100 g

Lesson 3: **Choosing suitable standard units: weight**

- Estimate and weigh in kilograms and grams, choosing the best unit

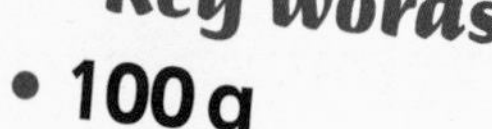

Key words
- **100 g**
- **1 kg**
- **estimate**
- **measure**
- **measuring instrument**

Discover

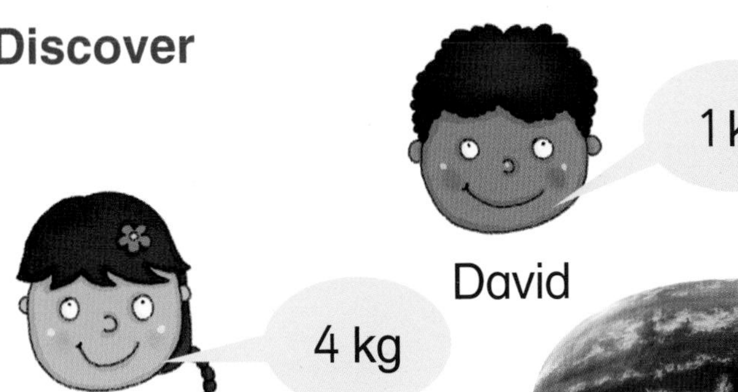

David

Suki

Misha

Kofi

Ali

Learn

You can choose the best unit to weigh something.

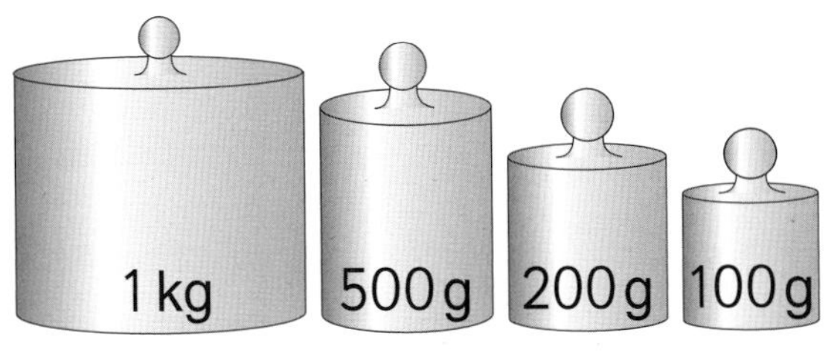

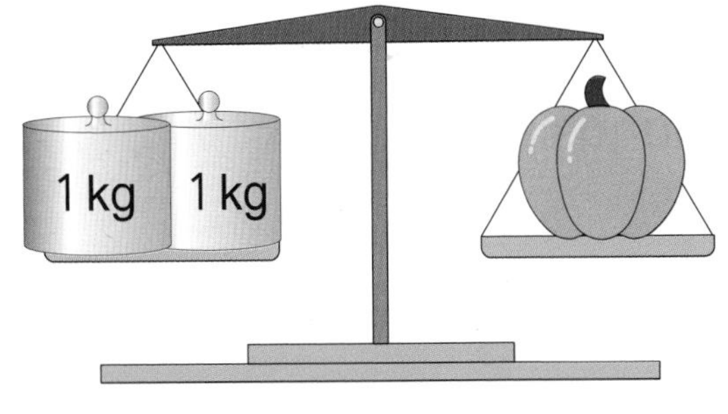

Weigh a heavy item in kg.

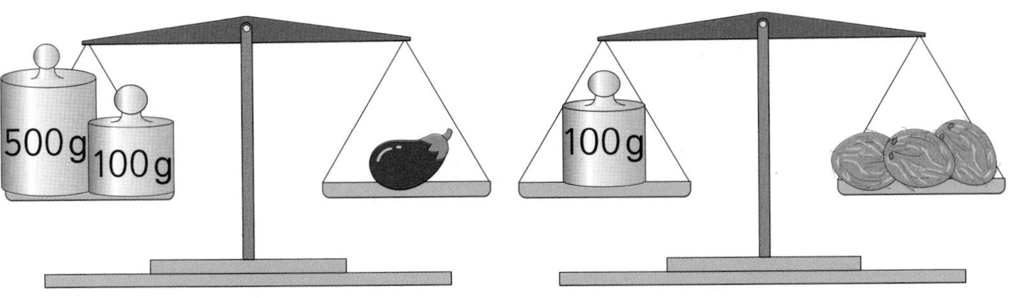

Weigh a lighter item in g.

Measure

Lesson 4: **Comparing weights**

- Compare weights in kilograms and grams

Key word

- **compare**
- **lighter**
- **lightest**
- **heavier**
- **heaviest**
- **gram (g)**
- **kilogram (kg)**

Discover

Learn

The watermelon is 1 kg heavier than the bananas.

The bananas are 1 kg lighter than the watermelon.

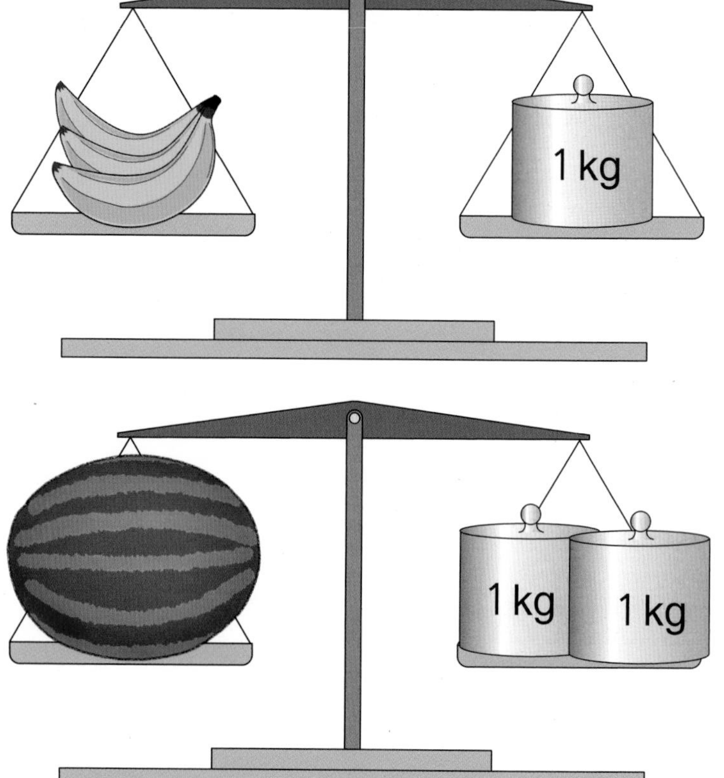

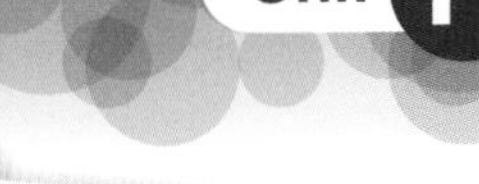

Lesson 1: **Measuring capacities using non-standard units**

- Estimate and measure capacity using units of measure that are the same

Key words
- capacity
- measure
- unit of measure

Discover

How many spadefuls of sand will it take to fill the bucket: 2, 20, 100 or 200?

Learn

Capacity is the measure of how much a container can hold.

Container being measured	Unit of measure
	 The capacity of the jug = 2 cups.
	 The capacity of the cup = 4 egg cups.

Measure

Lesson 2: **The litre (*l*)**

- Recognise more than, less than and a whole litre on a measuring instrument

Key words
- **litre (*l*)**
- **more than, >**
- **less than, <**

Discover

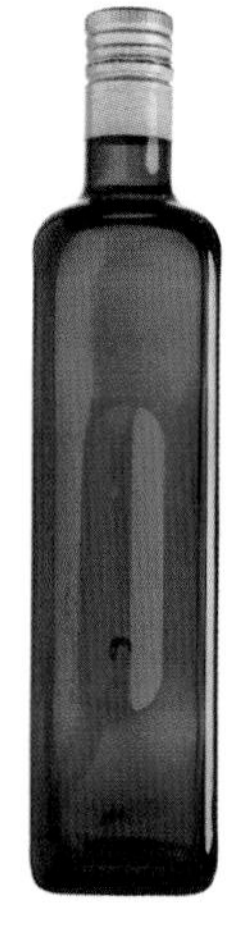

1 litre | 1 litre | 1 litre | 1 litre

Learn

less than 1 litre

1 litre

more than 1 litre

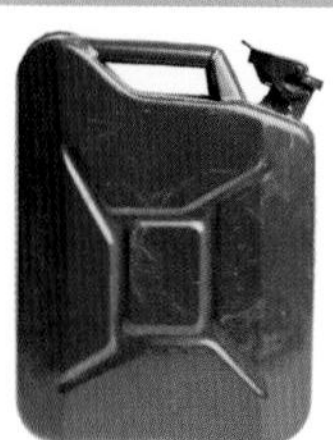

Lesson 3: **Measuring capacities using standard units**

- Estimate and measure capacity in litres

Key words
- estimate
- measure
- litre (l)
- more than, >
- less than, <

Discover

Container	Less than 1l	About 1l	More than 1l
	✓		
		✓	
			✓

Learn

I estimate that the cooking pot holds 2 litres and that the carton of milk holds 1 litre.

2 litres

1 litre

Lesson 4: **Comparing capacities using standard units**

- Use litres to compare capacities

Key words

- compare
- measure
- litre (l)
- more than, >
- less than, <

Discover

Learn

Be capacity detectives. Compare containers with the same unit of measure, litres. Compare the capacity of different 1 l capacity containers.

The jug's capacity is more than a litre.

capacity > 1 litre

Lesson 1: **The units of time**

- Know different units of time and order the months by name

Key words
- second
- minute
- hour
- day
- week
- month
- year

Discover

January February March April May June July August September October November December

Learn

1 year: 12 months, 52 weeks

1 week: 7 days

1 day: 24 hours

1 hour: 60 minutes

1 minute: 60 seconds

Lesson 2: **Reading the time to the half hour**

- Read half past the hour in digital numbers and on a clock face

Key words
- digital
- half past
- clockwise
- minute hand
- 30 minutes

Discover

Learn

To Past

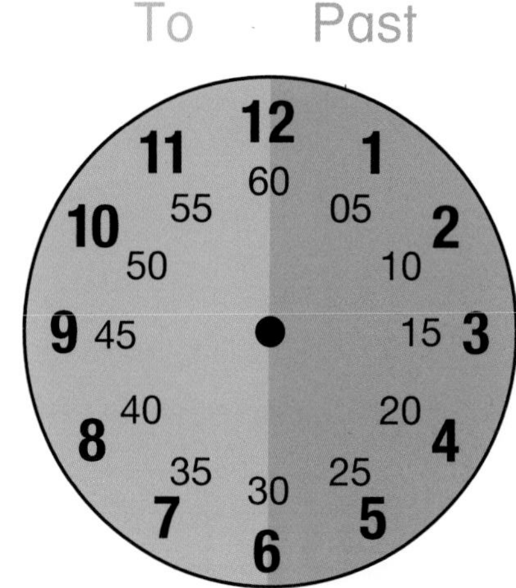

4:30

3:30

7:30

Lesson 3: **Showing the time to the half hour**

- Write half past in digital time, and mark the hands on a clock

Key words

- **half past the hour**
- **30 minutes**

Discover

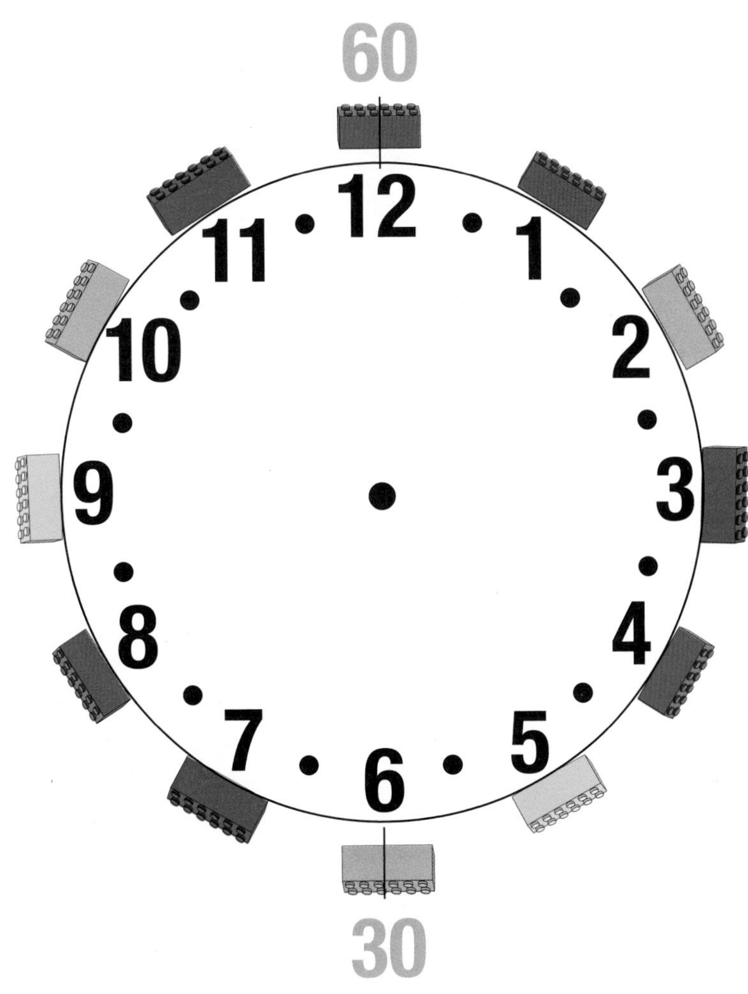

Learn

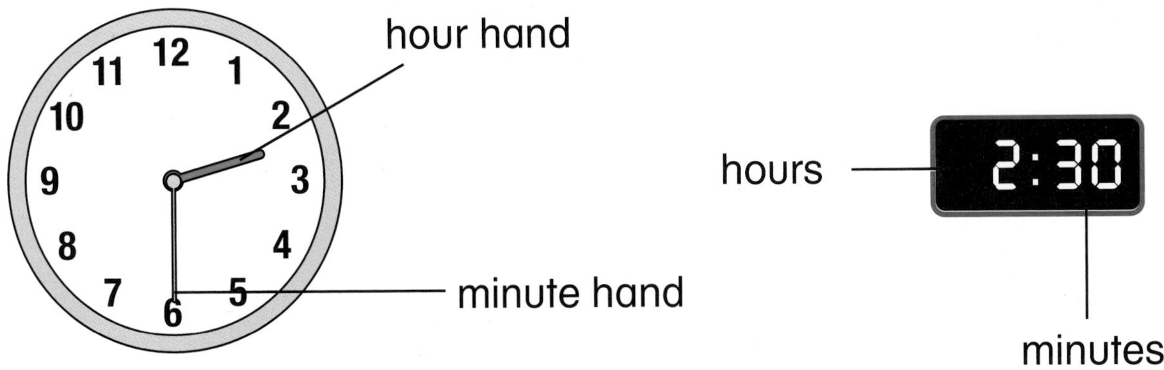

Lesson 4: **Measuring time**

- Use familiar words to measure time

Key words
- second
- minute
- hour
- day
- week
- month
- year

Discover

Learn

One second has passed.

One minute has passed.

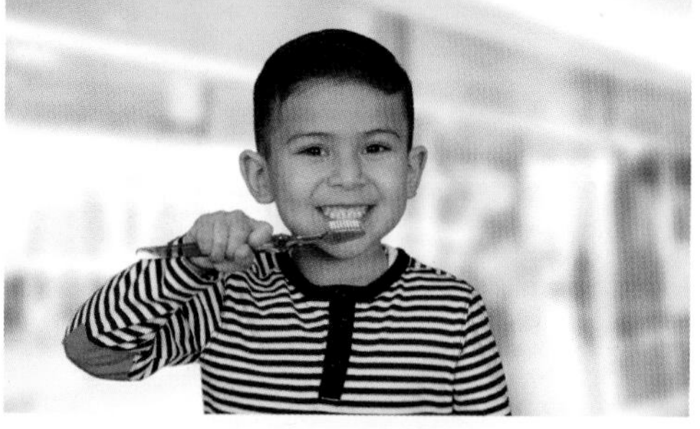

It can take months for a new tooth to grow.

Lesson 1: **Data in lists and tables**

- Collect, record and read information in lists and tables

Key words
- list
- table
- title
- heading
- row

Discover

How could you sort the food packaging?

Learn

Data can be shown in different ways:

- 4 plums
- 6 apples
- 3 onions
- 5 bananas
- 1 melon

Item	Number
plum	4
apple	6
onion	3
banana	5
melon	1

Example

Food on the shopping list.

Fruit and vegetables	Other items
bananas carrots pears	milk bread chicken

Lesson 2: **Carroll and Venn diagrams with one sorting rule**

- Read and create Carroll and Venn diagrams with one sorting rule

Key words

- **Carroll diagram**
- **Venn diagram**
- **sorting rule**

Discover

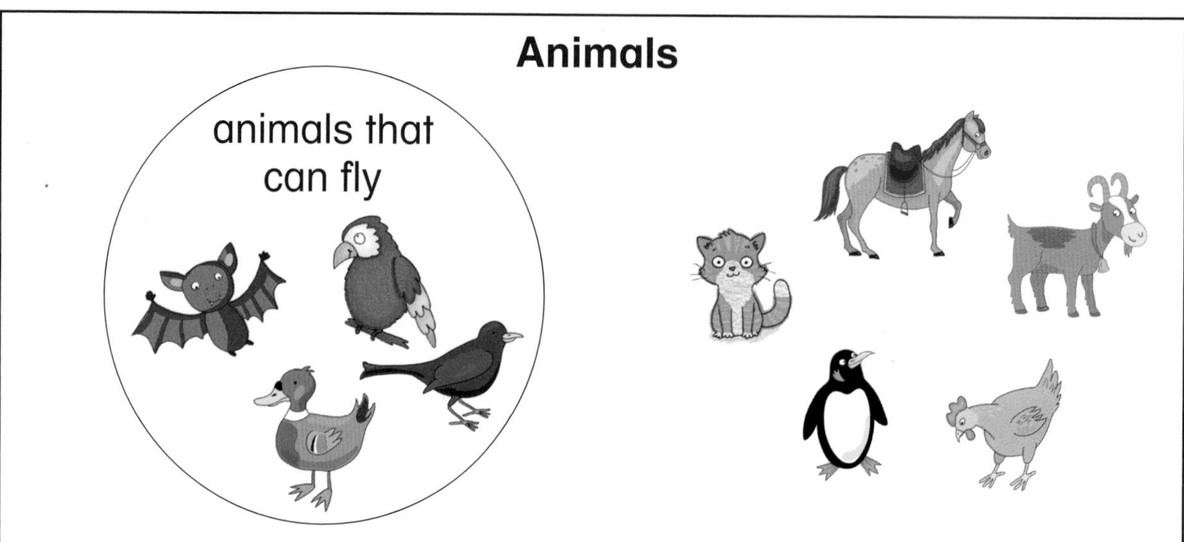

Learn

A Venn diagram:

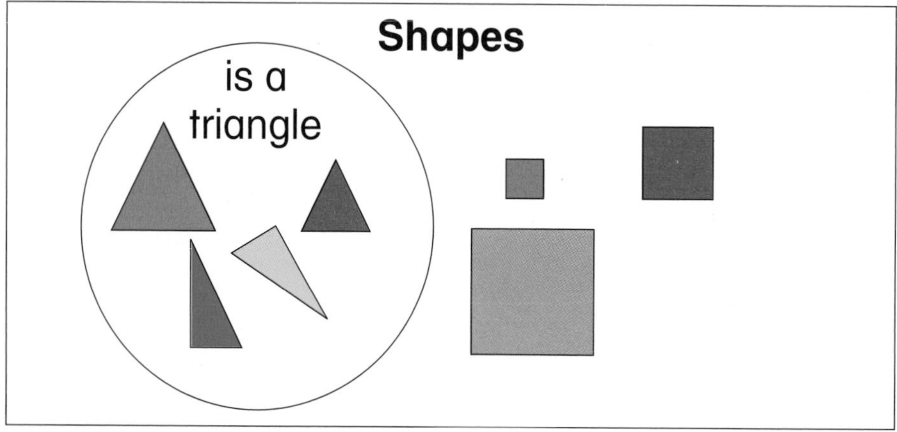

A Carroll diagram.

Shapes

is a triangle	is not a triangle

Lesson 3: Carroll diagrams with two sorting rules

- Read and create Carroll diagrams with two sorting rules

Key words
- Carroll diagram
- sorting rule
- title
- heading
- row

Discover

Is there more than one sorting rule?

Birds that can fly

	is a bird	is not a bird
can fly		
cannot fly		

Learn

Boys that have brown hair

	is a boy	is not a boy
has brown hair		
does not have brown hair		

Lesson 4: Venn diagrams with two sorting rules

- Read and create Venn diagrams with two sorting rules

Key words
- **Venn diagram**
- **sorting rule**
- **title**

Discover

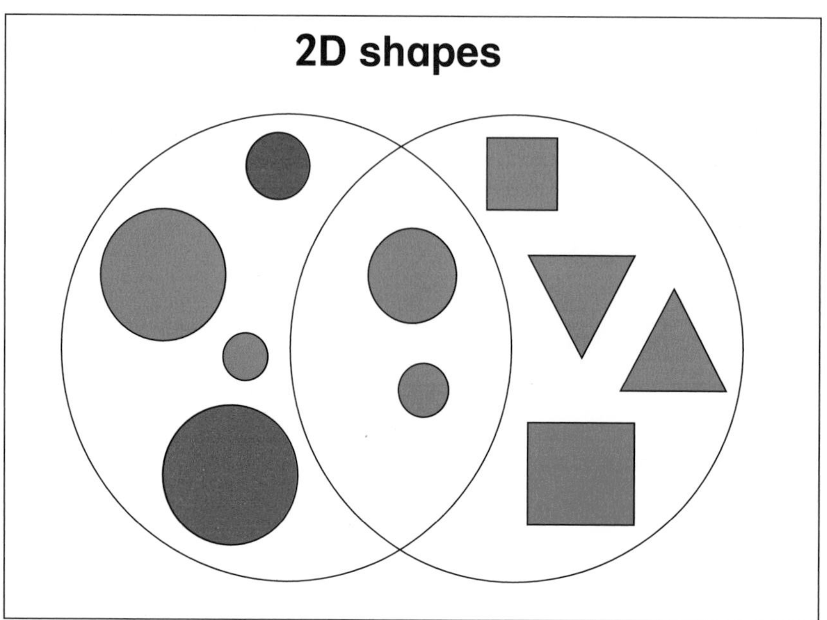

Learn

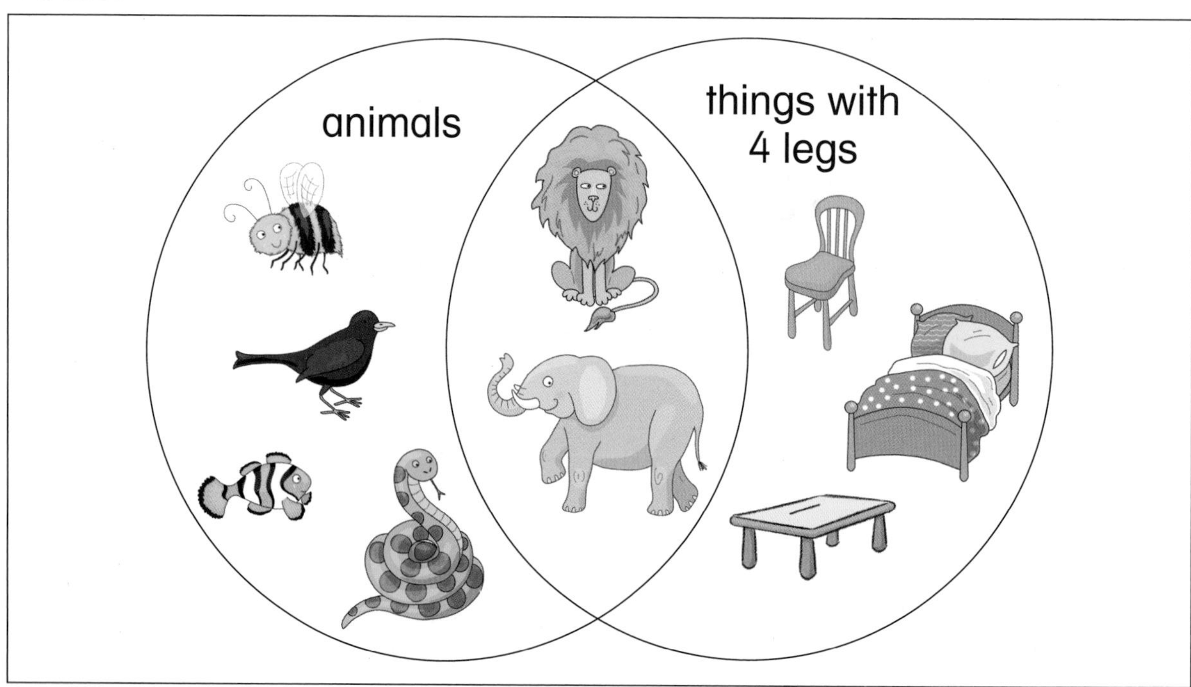

Lesson 5: Block graphs

- Collect, record and read information on a block graph

Key words
- block graph
- value

Discover

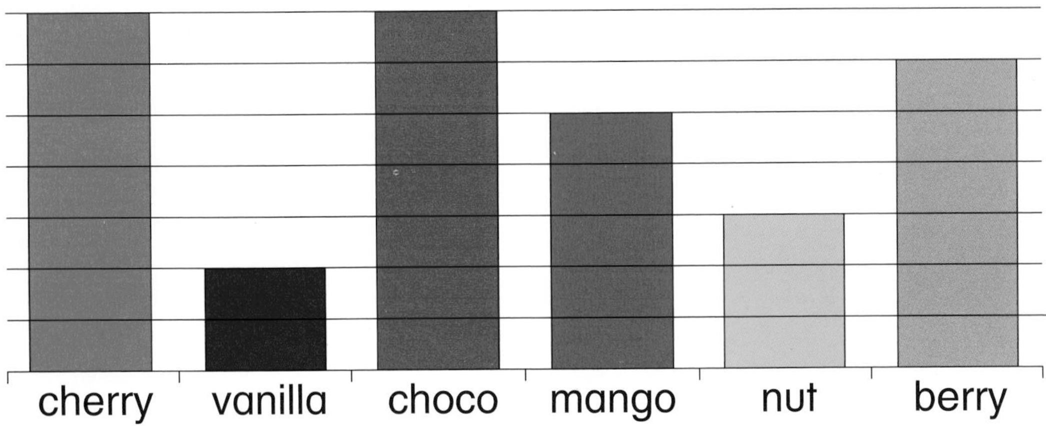

Learn

Animals on a farm

Animal	Number
cow	2
sheep	3
goat	4
chicken	7

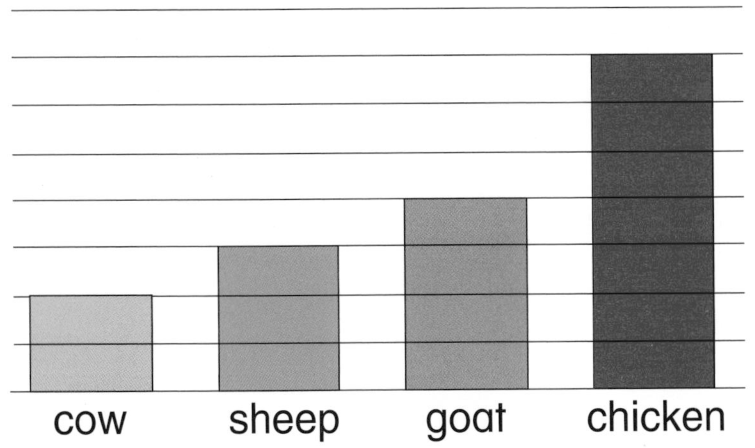

Lesson 6: **Pictograms**

- Collect, record and read information on a pictogram

Key word
- **pictogram**

Discover

Learn

This pictogram shows how many of each vehicle drove past the school in one hour.

Vehicles going past the school in 1 hour

car 

truck 

bus 

motorbike 

bicycle 

Lesson 7: **Collecting, recording and interpreting data (1)**

Key word
- survey

- Ask a question and conduct a survey, showing results in a graph

Discover

Learn

First, ask a question.

Then collect the information.

Flavour	Number
chocolate	7
lemon	3
cherry	6
vanilla	1

What is your favourite cake flavour?

Show the information in a diagram.

Favourite cake

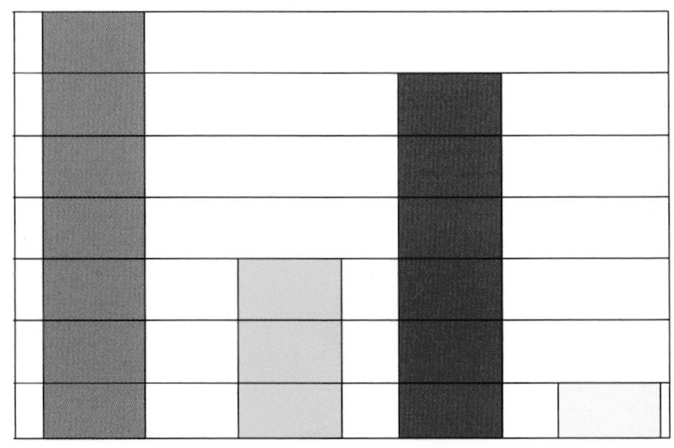

7 children like chocolate!

Lesson 8: **Collecting, recording and interpreting data (2)**

- Ask a question and conduct a survey, showing results in a diagram

Key word
- question
- survey
- Carroll diagram
- Venn diagram

Discover

Learn

Ask a question, collect results and show the data.

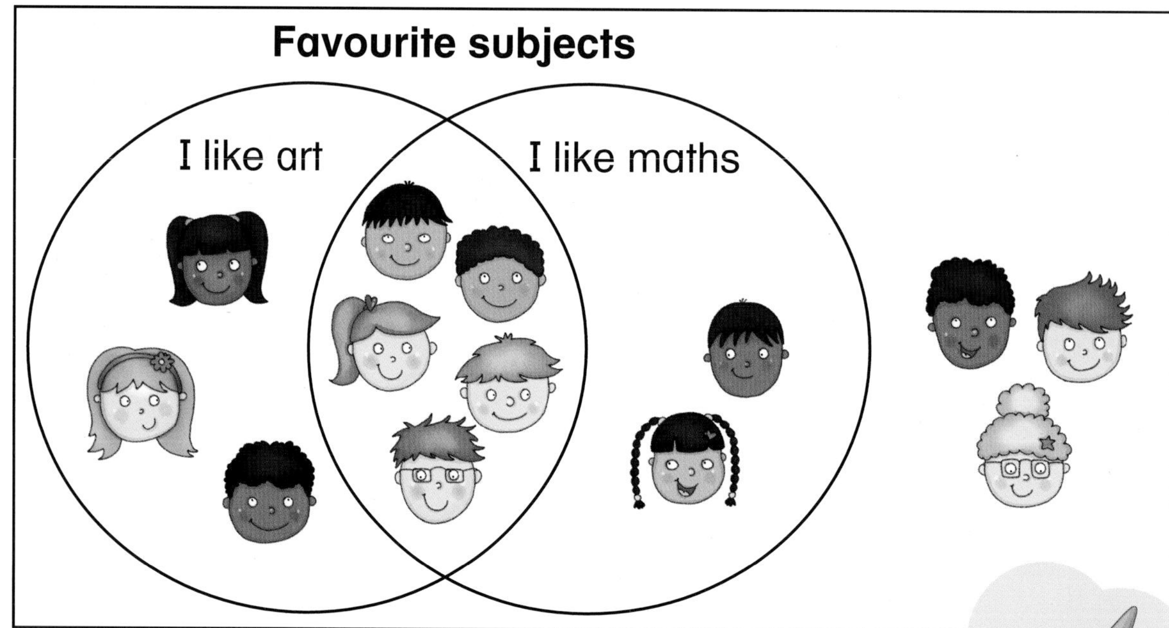

	likes maths	does not like maths
likes art	5	3
does not like art	2	3

Notes

Notes

Notes

Notes